CW00894432

Drink to Your Health

Harper's
MAGAZINE PRESS

Drink to Your Health

Alcohol Without Alcoholism
by Junius Adams

Harper's Magazine Press
Published in Association with
Harper & Row, New York

To Carole, with love and gratitude

"Harper's" is the registered trademark of Harper & Row, Publishers, Inc.

Drink to Your Health. Copyright © 1976 by Junius Adams. All rights reserved. Printed in the United States of America. No part of this book may be used or reproduced in any manner whatsoever without written permission except in the case of brief quotations embodied in critical articles and reviews: For information address Harper & Row, Publishers, Inc., 10 East 53rd Street, New York, N.Y. 10022. Published simultaneously in Canada by Fitzhenry & Whiteside Limited, Toronto.

FIRST EDITION

Library of Congress Cataloging in Publication Data

Adams, Junius.
  Drink to Your Health.

  Bibliography: p.
  Includes index.
  1. Alcoholism. 2. Alcohol—Physiological
effect. 3. Alcoholics. I. Title.
HV5035.A3   362.2'92   75-9358
ISBN 0-06-120030-1

76 77 78 79 10 9 8 7 6 5 4 3 2 1

Grateful acknowledgment is made for permission to reprint the following material:

Excerpt from *Prejudices: A Selection* by H. L. Mencken edited by James T. Farrell. Copyright © 1958 by Alfred A. Knopf, Inc. Reprinted by permission of Alfred A. Knopf, Inc.

Excerpt from *Nutrition Against Disease* by Roger J. Williams. Copyright © 1971 by Pitman Publishing Corporation. Reprinted by permission of Pitman Publishing Corp.

Excerpt from *Love and Addiction* by Stanton Peele with Archie Brodsky. Copyright © 1975 by Stanton Peele and Archie Brodsky. Published by Taplinger Publishing Co., Inc., New York.

Excerpt from *Vitamins in Your Life* by Erwin DiCyan. Copyright © 1972, 1975 by Erwin DiCyan. Reprinted by permission of Simon & Schuster, Inc.

Excerpt from *The Disease Concept of Alcoholism* by E. M. Jellinek. Reprinted by permission of Hillhouse Press.

Excerpt from *Alcohol and Civilization* by S. P. Lucia. Published by McGraw-Hill Book Co.

Excerpt from *Overweight: Causes, Cost and Control* by Jean Mayer (pp. 72, 82). Reprinted by permission of Prentice-Hall, Inc., Englewood Cliffs, New Jersey.

Excerpt from *Total Fitness in 30 Minutes a Week* by Laurence E. Moorehouse, Ph.D. and Leonard Gross. Copyright © 1975 by Laurence E. Moorehouse, Ph.D. Reprinted by permission of Simon & Schuster, Inc.

Excerpt from *W. C. Fields: His Fortunes and Follies* by Robert Lewis Taylor. Copyright 1949, © 1967 by Robert Lewis Taylor. Reprinted by permission of the author.

Excerpt from *Liquor, the Servant of Man* by Walton Hall Smith and Ferdinand C. Helwig, M.D. Reprinted by permission of Little, Brown and Co.

Excerpt from *Prohibition: The Era of Excess* by Andrew Sinclair. Copyright © 1962 by Andrew Sinclair. Reprinted by permission of Little, Brown & Co.

Contents

Foreword

ALCOHOL, in the western world, is the one drug that is both "respectable" and universally available. Most adults drink, and countless millions of them do so to a degree beyond what could be considered moderate. There are no restrictions on alcohol, no labels proclaiming it "hazardous to your health." Yet these hazards do exist, and it would seem reasonable that any regular drinker should want to know exactly what risks he is assuming as he's imbibing his nightly cocktails.

To convey this information is not an easy task, however. Although the immediate physiological effects of alcohol are well known, we still do not have a proper understanding of the consequences of long-term use. Medical science today is barely becoming aware of the many toxic and pathologic changes caused by alcohol. Certainly medicine has known cirrhosis and encephalopathy for centuries, but it is only in recent times that we recognize the pathologic changes in the heart and muscle systems and the extensive injury to the brain and nervous system. It is only within the last few years that a research model of cirrhosis has been produced in order that cirrhosis could finally be properly studied. Perhaps some day medical science will be able to inform the public about how much alcohol is safe for each person and how much is too much, but present knowledge does not allow us to do so with any exactitude. There are great variations in individual susceptibility to drink. Some of us are more vulnerable than others and require much smaller amounts of alcohol to induce serious pathology. Some, on the other hand, seem to be highly resistant and are able to survive into ripe old age while consuming quantities that would be, over a long period, lethal for the average person. We have as yet no means of identifying or predicting these levels of vulnerability.

Still, since so many of us find pleasure in drinking and will continue to do so despite all warnings and scare stories, we ought to know the currently understood facts about alcohol and its effect on the body and thereby develop some guidelines of safety. In this book, Junius Adams has made a systematic attempt to inform the regular drinker of the current available facts and to acquaint him as well with various theories and possibilities which are still under investigation. While offering specific advice and definite recommendations, Mr. Adams also presents information which will help the reader decide for himself how much he ought to drink, and how often.

For the reader sincerely interested in evaluating his own relationship to alcohol, I would offer a word of caution: Keep in mind one serious error that is made by virtually all drinkers. When subjectively trying to estimate how much and how often they drink, they consistently underestimate both frequency and quantity. Often the person most vulnerable to alcohol is the one who is convinced he has no problem with it and is consuming only modest amounts, although the exact reverse is true.

Because of the many reasons we have for using it, we have made alcohol into a complex and protean substance. It can be a stimulant, sedative, tranquilizer, crutch, releaser of social inhibition, escape mechanism, aphrodisiac or creator of impotence, depending on who uses it and how and why it is used. The key to mature use of alcohol is to know yourself, know your own health, and know what effects drinking has on you. Then you can decide what, for you, constitutes safe drinking.

ELLIOTT J. HOWARD, M.D.

Fellow, American College of Physicians,
American College of Cardiology
Medical Director, Foundation for
Study of Exercise Stress and the Heart

Introduction

THIS IS a book for drinkers about drinking, by a drinker. It attempts to answer many questions drinkers often wonder about, such as: How bad is alcohol for my health? What can I do for a hangover? Am I turning into an alcoholic? How much booze is it safe to drink? Should I take vitamins? What's the best way to cut down when you're drinking too much? I've tried to track down authoritative answers to these questions and in general to furnish information that might lead, for some, to happier and healthier drinking.

In giving medical and physiological data, I've tried to find the latest information possible and also to rely whenever possible on sources that are unimpeachable—Dr. Roger J. Williams, of the Clayton Foundation Biochemical Institute, on nutrition and alcohol, Dr. Jean Mayer, Professor of Nutrition at Harvard University, on problems of overweight, Dr. Milton Helpern, former Chief Medical Examiner of New York City, on evidences of brain and muscle damage in alcoholics, among others.

I started this book assuming that I could get all the information I needed from experts or the writings of experts. In other words, it was going to be one of those medical-science-says reports that have become so popular with readers in recent years. I discovered very quickly, however, that on the subject of alcohol many of the "experts" are wrong. There are *not* nine million alcoholics in this country, for instance. All drunken drivers are *not* a menace on the highway. Heavy drinkers do *not* necessarily drink because of guilt, neurosis or insecurity, or to escape intolerable tensions or cover up emotional pain.

To find out something, one has to go to the proper source. If you want to know why people drink and what happens to them when they do, don't go to some scholarly theoretician who has studied a lot of psychiatric and medical reports on alcoholism; go ask some drinkers. I spent a year interviewing every healthy, hard-drinking adult I could find. Their experiences and insights have been invaluable.

I wanted this book to be a straightforward, factual health manual for normal moderate-to-heavy social drinkers, telling them everything they needed to know in order to stay healthy while drinking. I hope it has turned out to be that, although it's not as straightforward as I had wished. Nothing concerning alcohol is very straightforward today.

In the early part of this century it was hard to find out anything factual about alcohol because everyone was either a "dry" or a "wet"—an advocate of prohibition or an opponent—with lies and distortions of fact abounding on both sides. Today, reliable information is still in short supply because a new dry movement has appeared—composed of doctors, psychiatrists, government officials, research personnel, welfare workers and others, all of whom are in the business of studying, diagnosing and treating the "alcoholic" and the "problem drinker." Alcoholism is a multi-billion-dollar growth industry, and the alcoholism establishment—those concerned with the study, control and treatment of alcoholics—want to see it grow even further. The alcoholism establishment encompasses and/or dominates most of those in the medical profession who are in any way concerned with treating drinkers or investigating the effects of alcohol, so that there is little interest in the non-alcoholic drinker and his health problems. If he has any problems at all, in fact, they will claim him as one of theirs.

It is because of all this that I've had to detour and include some rather cynical thoughts about politics, alcoholism, public opinion, the medical profession and other matters, thoughts which will no doubt outrage and infuriate many interested parties but not, I hope, *you,* dear reader.

JUNIUS ADAMS

New York City
August 15, 1975

1

When You Take a Drink

ALCOHOL IS a versatile and unusual substance. It is a food, containing as many calories, seven per gram, as fat. It is an intoxicating, consciousness-altering drug. And, in large enough quantities, it is a poison which can produce death.

To get an idea of what alcohol does in the body, let's imagine that you're about to swallow a slug of straight whiskey or brandy. Before the liquor touches your lips, you've probably inhaled some of its fumes. That inhalation reaches the lungs and is absorbed into the blood. You now have a tiny trace of alcohol in your bloodstream.* Once swallowed, the liquor begins to be absorbed into the blood through the walls of the stomach. Unlike most other foods, alcohol does not need to be digested for the body to use it. It goes to work directly, in its original form. About 20 percent will be absorbed through the stomach, the rest through the small intestine. Alcohol diffuses very rapidly throughout all the body fluids; just a few minutes after you drink, it will be present in every part of your organism, including the bones.

If you took your drink on an empty stomach, its progress through the body would be swift—which is why one drink before dinner often seems to pack more wallop than two or three afterward. Food in the stomach, especially fatty or oily

*It's not just tiny amounts that can be absorbed this way: A persevering person can get quite smashed by inhaling brandy fumes from a snifter glass. One can also absorb alcohol (via enema) through the rectum. Taken rectally, alcohol hits very fast and relatively small amounts will produce drunkenness. The conventional route through the stomach is actually the most inefficient means of ingestion.

When You Take a Drink | 1

foods, will slow down the absorption process. Beer contains food substances which inhibit absorption: the same quantity of alcohol taken in the form of beer or ale will be less intoxicating than when taken as distilled spirits. In other beverages (such as whiskey-and-soda, champagne or sparkling wines) the presence of carbon-dioxide bubbles serves to speed the progress of alcohol, because the action of the bubbles tickles the pyloric valve, an organ which monitors the passage of material from the stomach to the intestine, causing it to open wide. This is why one has the feeling of getting drunker more quickly from champagne and other sparkling beverages. On the other hand, if you drink too-large amounts of liquor too quickly, the pylorus will go into spasm, shutting tightly. Nausea and vomiting ensue. This phenomenon probably accounts, at least in part, for the nausea and dizziness usually experienced by neophyte drinkers. The pyloric spasm and ensuing vomiting protects them against ingesting larger amounts of alcohol than their tissue tolerance allows.

As your drink is absorbed in the stomach and small intestine, the veins carry it to the liver, then through the right ventricle of the heart, then to the lungs (where some of it seeps out, giving you "alcohol breath") then to the aorta and from there throughout the body in the arterial circulation. When it reaches the brain alcohol produces its most significant effect, the one most of us drink it for: an anesthetic action which dulls the higher centers. Although this is a sedative effect, it feels like stimulation at first. The first drink or two relax the higher brain, bringing a mildly euphoric relaxation of psychic and physical tension. Along with this comes a feeling of warmth, caused by a slight elevation of pulse rate and blood pressure. Blood rushes into the capillaries, dilating them, and this in turn warms the skin.

This is a peripheral warming effect only—liquor causes a heat *loss*, actually, by bringing warmth to the surface of the body and thus dissipating it more rapidly than usual. Blood pressure, initially raised by the increased action of the heart, now becomes reduced as the blood vessels expand.

About 10 percent of the alcohol in the body is eliminated through the urine and the breath. The rest has to be oxidized (digested). Whereas food substances such as sugar or fat can be oxidized by tissues throughout the body, alcohol is digested only in the liver, a drop or two at a time. The average liver oxidizes approximately one-half ounce per hour—the equivalent of an ounce of 100-proof spirits. The alcohol is first converted to acetaldehyde, a rather toxic substance, which is in turn quickly converted to acetate, a basic energy source which can be used by all the body tissues. When the acetate is then oxidized, the final products are water and carbon dioxide.

Since the maximum amount of alcohol that can be eliminated by the body is about one-half ounce per hour, any amount more than this is retained in the body, causing drunkenness, which increases with the amounts ingested. The mechanism by which alcohol affects the brain to produce intoxication has never been fully understood, but the stages of drunkenness are. The first few doses of booze produce a mild anesthesia in the higher or "new" brain—that section which controls the function Freudians refer to as the superego. This part of the brain appears to contain and generate messages pertaining to caution, self-criticism, self-doubt, anxiety, oversensitivity to social pressures and exigencies, overreaction to pain, and so on. This initial anesthesia (let's call it the one-to-three-drink effect, allowing for individual differences in body weight, tolerance and reaction to alcohol) makes the drinker feel warm, mentally relaxed, often better able to display his skills and wit, less concerned with pain, irritations, inhibitions or restraints. More booze will further dampen the higher centers, producing an obvious relaxation of inhibitions, euphoria (though sometimes nastiness or moroseness), exaggerated emotion, displays of amorousness, aggression or outrageous humor. Let's call this the two-to-six-drink effect.

At this point the higher brain centers are decidedly depressed. More liquor will now begin to affect those centers which control motor functions. The four-to-ten-drink effect consists of clumsiness and impaired coordination, unsteadiness in walking or standing, and a tendency to primitive, gross, uncouth or uncontrollable behavior (the higher brain is virtually asleep now). Still more liquor will produce obvious incoordination of the motor functions, with considerable stumbling and falling down and mental impairment to the point of incoherence. With another drink or two, the person will almost invariably pass out in a semi-stupor. If he ingests still more alcohol, he will fall into a state of general anesthesia or coma. A really large additional dose will produce death by anesthetizing that part of the brain that controls respiration. This lethal effect of alcohol, by stopping respiration, is identical to the lethal effects of other anesthetic agents, such as opiates, barbiturates or ether. Cases of death by drinking are fortunately rare. Habitual drunks, accustomed as they are to ingesting huge amounts of alcohol, sometimes manage to take one last lethal dose just before passing out. Other deaths occur as the result of a bet: a show-off drinker will wager that he can drink x amount of drinks within y number of minutes and will drop dead after his performance. His mistake was not in the amount of liquor consumed—ordinarily he could probably handle it—but in the precipitateness with which he drank. When you gulp liquor instead of sipping it, the effects are much more severe.

How Drunk Is Drunk?

Body weight and blood alcohol levels

The amount of alcohol present in the blood is often used as an indicator of how much liquor a person has ingested and thus, presumably, of how drunk he is. The official abbreviation for this is BAC, or blood alcohol concentration. Sometimes the breath or urine is tested instead; the resulting figure will be identical with the BAC, since alcohol is diffused equally throughout the body fluids. Here are the approximate BACs for the states of intoxication discussed above.

Blood Alcohol Concentration	Effect
.05% (5 parts per 10,000)	Slight changes in feeling and consciousness
.10%	Euphoria, garrulousness, perhaps some clumsiness
.15%	Definite intoxication
.20–.25%	"Falling-down-drunk"
.30–.40%	Stupor
.40–.55%	Coma
.60% or over	Usually fatal

Obviously, since the BAC is an index of how much alcohol is present in the body fluids, the amount of alcohol required to produce a given BAC depends on the size of the individual. Someone weighing 120 pounds will require only half as much alcohol as someone of 240 pounds to achieve the same BAC. And, since a woman's body is made up of only 55–65 percent water, as opposed to 65–75 percent for a man, women need less liquor than men to reach the same BAC. Here, according to body weight, are the numbers of drinks required to reach a given state. (A drink is one ounce of 100-proof spirits or 1¼ ounces of 80-proof.)

BAC OF .05%

Weight (pounds)	Number of drinks
100	one and a fraction
120	scant two
140	two
160	two
180	scant three
200	scant three
220	three
240	three

BAC OF .10%

100	scant three
120	three and a fraction

Weight (pounds)	Number of drinks
140	scant four
160	four and a fraction
180	scant five
200	scant six
220	six
240	scant seven

BAC OF .15%

100	four
120	scant five
140	scant six
160	scant seven
180	seven
200	eight
220	nine
240	scant ten

These figures apply to amounts of booze ingested within a relatively short time—one to two hours. Notice the dramatic difference according to size: The four drinks that will make the 100-pound person fully sloshed have scarcely an effect on the 240-pounder. Reverse this and give the 100-pounder the ten drinks required to make the big person drunk and the small person would be practically comatose, with a .40 percent BAC. This is why the practice of having drinks in "rounds" is either unfair to the large person, who can barely get a glow on if the pace of drinking is geared to the smallest drinker—or disastrous to the small person, who will get totally blotto while trying to keep up with drinkers twice his size.

What tends to happen in hard-drinking social groups, however, is much less arithmetical than the charts above, especially for the lighter-weight drinkers. In my interviews with drinkers, a number of men weighing 190–200 pounds or more reported that 10 to 12 drinks during a party or evening of drinking was their normal limit—more than that would make them too drunk and cause them to have hangovers the next day. Several 95–120-pound women said *their* limit was 6 to 8 drinks, relatively a much heavier consumption than for the men. Evidently they had developed considerably more tolerance for alcohol than had the men.

The two types of tolerance

If you serve someone who has never drunk before several drinks of liquor, he/she will probably show all the signs of advanced intoxication: dizziness and incoordination, maudlin or extravagant behavior, perhaps also nausea and vomiting. This may seem like a purely physiological reaction but it is not; the same thing happens to people getting high on marijuana for the first time. Both groups cannot handle the flood of new sensations assaulting their consciousness, and respond in an exaggerated way (like a "drunken sailor"). It is the consciousness-altering characteristics that produce such uncontrolled reactions.

After the neophyte drinker has had more experience, he no longer reacts so quickly, and can remain relatively sober on two or three times the alcohol that rendered him helpless during his first few drinking experiences. If he now goes on to become a seasoned drinker who can "hold his liquor," he will be able to act and talk with seeming sobriety while maintaining a BAC that would put less-experienced drinkers under the table. The drunken state is a new mode of existence that can be learned. Just as a newborn baby, unable at first to coordinate any of his movements, learns eventually to grasp with his hands, then stand up, then walk and talk, then operate computers or space vehicles, so the drunk, given sufficient experience, can learn to cope with his state. In his vaudeville days, for instance, W. C. Fields was able to perform six acts daily of intricate jugglery while on a one-to-two-quarts-of-gin-per-day drinking regime. Fields had "learned" the drunken state and could function within it.

This type of acquired tolerance is referred to as *psychological* or *behavioral* tolerance. It is the main form of habituation that drinkers acquire. Chronic extra-heavy drinkers can also acquire *tissue tolerance.* In experiments with heavy drinkers, Drs. Jack H. Mendelson and Joseph La Dou of Harvard Medical School discovered that "when subjects were receiving 30 oz. [of liquor] per 24 hr. the degree of intoxication was surprisingly small. Similarly, the serum alcohol levels were lower than would be expected." In other words, the bodies of chronic heavy drinkers have found ways to metabolize alcohol more efficiently than is usual. That tissue tolerance does exist is corroborated by the fact that ultra-heavy drinkers also show a "cross-resistance" to anesthetics such as ether and chloroform. As the well-known authority on alcoholism, Dr. E. M. Jellinek, says, "It is the common experience of surgeons that alcoholic patients require much more of these substances than do others in order to produce surgical anesthesia." Tissue tolerance does not extend very far. Dr. Mendelson found that the same subjects who thrived on 30 ounces per day had trouble when their dosage was increased to 40 ounces. Dr. Mendelson suggests that for men there may be a sort of natural limit of one quart per day which it is dangerous to go beyond. The same notion was mentioned to me by several of the heavy drinkers I interviewed. (Perhaps the same holds true for women. In her alcoholic memoir, *I'll Cry Tomorrow,* Lillian Roth mentions that the worst period of her life was when she was drinking a quart of whiskey every morning, and a quart every night. That second quart was 32 ounces too much.)

The up curve and the down curve

Liquor feels a lot better while it's taking effect than while it's wearing off—especially if you're having "more than one." A person getting high feels exhilarated, confident, relaxed, energetic—he's getting the stimulant effect of alcohol. Coming down from his high, he's apt to feel logy, drowsy and out of sorts—the depressant effects are now revealed. When I was a magazine editor and had frequent business lunches, many of them two-to-three-martini ones, I grew to dread those afternoons that followed my overly-alcoholic noon hours. My energy would be low, it was an effort to concentrate on the work before me, and in general I felt useless and inefficient, like someone forced to stay up past his bedtime. I was suffering, in effect, a mini-hangover. Had I not been at work, I would probably—as I've done occasionally on nonworking days such as weekends or vacations—have continued to tipple, enough to stay "up," then observed the cocktail hour, followed by a gloriously sloshy dinner and an early bedtime—a much comfier way to handle the midday alcoholic blues.

Actually, though I *felt* dopey during my post-drinking afternoons, I was able to perform rather intricate work—correcting mind-boggling lapses of grammar or logic in a troublesome manuscript or deleting 117 lines from a set of galleys without disturbing the continuity of the article—quite adequately. This is one of the deceptive aspects of the drinking experience. On his up curve, the drinker feels he is gloriously alive and capable; on the down, he feels inept and zombie-esque. Yet actually the reverse is true, as can be demonstrated by experiment. Drs. Ben Morgan Jones and Oscar A. Parsons, of the University of Oklahoma Health Sciences Center, for instance, tested a group of drinkers with a series of verbal puzzles and found that their performance was more impaired "while transcending into the alcohol state than while sinking back to earth." In another study they found that drinkers had poorer short-term memories while getting drunk than while sobering up, even when their blood alcohol levels were the same.

Is the cocktail hour ordained by our biological clock?

Although I like martinis, I couldn't possibly take one in the morning—just before breakfast, say—the very thought is nauseating. Before lunch, a martini is possible, though the first sip or two give me an involuntary shudder, as if my body were not quite ready yet. At the cocktail hour, however, the prospect of a martini is totally inviting. I'm ready for it. Is this just a matter of habit, social conditioning? Probably not.

In her book *Body Time,* Gay Gaer Luce tells about an experiment in which mice were injected with a quantity of alcohol equivalent to one quart of vodka for a human being. When the mice were given the alcohol early in the day, around their usual time of awakening, 60 percent of them died. The same dose given as a nightcap, close to their time of rest, killed only 12 percent. Not totally conclusive, perhaps, but I believe that more or less the same pattern holds true for human beings. The person who waits until sundown to start drinking is more in tune with the tides of life than the one who starts first thing in the morning.

Legal drunkenness and how to avoid it

In most of the states of the union—44 to be exact—you are considered legally drunk if your blood alcohol concentration exceeds .10 percent. Idaho and Utah are stricter: their limit is .08 percent. More generous to drinkers are Maryland, Mississippi, New Jersey and Wisconsin (also Puerto Rico): they allow .15 percent. Mostly these legal definitions are used to determine (via breath analysis or blood test) whether you are guilty of drunken driving. Here are some figures to show approximately how much you can drink without becoming guilty of drunkenness.

.10% LIMIT

Body Weight (pounds)	Number of Drinks (within a 2-to-4-hour period)
100	3
120	4
140	4
160	5

180	5
200	6
220	6
240	7

(To make the .08% limit, use the above figures, but leave a smidgen in the bottom of each glass.)

.15% LIMIT

100	4
120	5
140	6
160	7
180	7
200	8
220	9
240	10

Stages of drunkenness

Since we're going to be discussing the various stages of drunkenness throughout this book, it's probably a good idea to define them right now so that we know what we're talking about. For our purposes, it will be sufficient to distinguish four different stages.

Stage One: Mild euphoria, slight relaxation of tensions and inhibitions, feelings of warmth and cheerfulness. No overt signs of drunkenness.

Stage Two: Marked relaxation of inhibitions, expansive, talkative, sociable, more or less noticeably "under the influence."

Stage Three: Definite drunkenness, with at least some clumsiness due to impaired motor functions. More or less unrestrained acting-out of sociable, aggressive or amorous impulses. Heightened emotionalism.

Stage Four: Befuddled condition, markedly clumsy, incoherent, semi-comatose.

It has often been stated that people drink because they like the personality changes that alcohol brings them. This notion is certainly borne out by my interviews with drinkers. Almost unanimously, they felt that being in Stage One or Stage Two gave them a personality or social presence which was more effective and pleasurable than their normal cold-sober one.

These stages of drunkenness can also be used to define different types of drinkers. The Stage One drinker is a moderate social drinker who enjoys the mildly relaxing effects of taking a drink or two but does not seek or relish drunkenness in any form. If the Stage One drinker takes a few too many and slides into Stage Two, he may have a feeling of having transgressed and of having made a fool of himself. He has no particular desire to lapse from sobriety.

The Stage Two drinker enjoys the expansiveness and seeming emotional freedom he finds in the semi-drunken state. He feels confident, witty, jovial, better able to express himself and to function in a group. Many Stage Two drinkers are people who find alcohol a help to them in their occupation: the salesman who discovers he can approach people more easily and deliver a better sales pitch with a few drinks under his belt, the jazz musician who finds he can play with more verve and attempt more daring improvisations, the night-club comic who finds it easier to make people laugh when he has consumed some bottled hilarity. Being in Stage Two can be helpful to people whose effectiveness is enhanced by heightened emotionalism and sociability or fancifulness and exaggeration in verbal communications. The writer, the actor, the political orator can often find inspiration in the bottle. Nuclear physicists, certified public accountants or diamond cutters are probably better advised to do their drinking outside of working hours.

The Stage Three drinker is someone who perhaps feels cut off from his deeper, more instinctual self, and finds that alcohol enables him to tap emotions and impulses that are not otherwise available to him. As one heavy drinker said to me, "It may be an illusion, but getting smashed makes me feel whole again. I can say what I really mean, feel what I really feel." Primitive societies for whom drinking is a religious ritual prize Stage Three as being a holy or ecstatic state. Perhaps our American contemporary drunks, getting together in some communal setting such as Bill's living room or McNulty's saloon and downing the booze until everyone gets darkly exalted or passionately portentous, are also unknowingly performing a religious ritual.

Stage Three encourages far-out or exhibitionist behavior. The drunk who steps out into a busy street and starts directing traffic, the woman who throws off her clothes and goes for a bathe in the Plaza fountain are Stage Three personalities. A number of drinkers reported to me that they like Stage Three because it inspires them sexually, making them more direct, passionate or flamboyant in bed.

The Stage Four drinker, or drunk, drinks in order to blot out consciousness entirely. This activity may represent a desire to return to the womb, as some psychoanalysts have suggested. Or it may simply be a quite understandable attempt to escape from present circumstances, as with the Skid Row bum who appears to be the most frequent Stage Four drinker. If I had to sleep in a depressing flophouse cubicle, or in a doorway under a blanket of newspapers, I think I too would wish to do so while comfortably blotto. Some Stage Four drinkers, of course, are respectably well-heeled citizens who drink themselves into extinction in the privacy of their own homes. Every heavy drinker experiences Stage Four at times, but the true Stage Four drinker is someone who habitually uses alcohol to achieve oblivion and gets there rather rapidly, without especially enjoying the first three stages.

For any given individual stages of drunkenness are, in effect, different personalities, exhibiting traits not necessarily found in the individual's sober personality. Someone who is normally polite, tactful and reserved, for instance, may become blunt, aggressive and outspoken in Stage Two or Stage Three. A normally kind and thoughtful person can become cold and unfeeling, just as a cold, repressive type may wax warm and solicitous. The more time a drinker spends in his alternate personality, the more that personality develops a life, character and history all its own. Research on what is called "state-dependent" learning suggests that this alternate personality phenomenon may be something that is common to all animal life. One researcher, Donald Overton, demonstrated that when rats are trained under the influence of a drug, they remember what they learned better when put back into the same drugged state than when undrugged or drugged with some other substance. The same experiment was done with humans, using alcohol as the drug, and the human subjects performed in the same way the rats did —when trained in a task after drinking alcohol, they remembered their training better after having drunk again than when sober.

The drunken millionaire in Charlie Chaplin's *City Lights* is a perfect example of the alternate personality phenomenon. When drunk, he feels Charlie is his great buddy; he lavishes presents on him, takes him out to night clubs, throws parties for him. But when he wakes up sober he has no memory of Chaplin and has him thrown out of the house. As soon as he is again drunk, Chaplin is again his dear friend.

The blackout

A drinker will have no difficulty remembering what happened while he was in Stage One, and seldom will forget his Stage Two experiences, but there will be memory lapses—ranging from slight to almost total—in Stage Three or Four drunkenness. In his movie *The Bank Dick,* W. C. Fields asks a bartender, "Was I in here last night, and did I spend a twenty-dollar bill?" On being told yes, Fields says, "Thank goodness, I thought I'd lost it!" Frequently drinkers cannot remember who drove them home the night before, how they got to bed, whether or not they had sex with their spouses, and so on. The more alcohol tolerance the drinker has built up, the more likely he is to have blackouts: he is able to remain on his feet and functioning after taking on a dose of alcohol that would put a less tolerant drinker to sleep. The blackout may obliterate scattered memories only, or it may cover hours and even days (a type of pathological memory lapse psychiatrists refer to as a "fugue"). A *New York Magazine* article on alcoholic New York City policemen describes one of these extended blackouts. A young patrolman came to in a hotel room in the Caribbean with a strange woman he had just married; his last memory was of going out to a bar in Queens for a couple of beers—over a week previously.

The blackout is similar to sleepwalking or the trance state. The conscious personality is asleep, and a secondary personality has taken over. Sometimes the blacked-out person will appear quite lucid and normal to the people around him, able to take part in group activities and engage in seemingly intelligent conversations, but the next day he will remember nothing. Having an extended blackout is often a spooky and unsettling experience. Many drinkers become quite frightened after "losing" a few hours the night before and take the pledge, seek psychiatric help, or join Alcoholics Anonymous. It is not a comfortable thought to realize that the self, the "I," is such a feeble construct that it can be obliterated by a pint or two of liquor, leaving the body under the control of what seems like an alien personality.

Why we drink "too much"

Light and moderate drinkers seldom have the problem of "involuntarily" drinking to excess, except perhaps on occasions when they are coerced into drunkenness by heavier-drinking companions. But the drinker who sets out to achieve Stage Two or Stage Three often does find that he continues drinking after he has reached his goal. The trouble is that, once he has reached a certain state of drunkenness, he is no longer the same *person* who had earlier decided, "I'll have three drinks—no more" or ". . . six drinks—no more." As an old Japanese proverb says,

"First the man takes a drink, then the drink takes a drink, then the drink takes the man."

Sober, the drinker has all his inhibitory mechanisms in working order. He can decide to take just one drink and stick to his decision. Deciding to take five drinks but not six poses problems, however. After the five drinks, he is not the sober fellow who resolved to be moderate. He's feeling elated, expansive, daring if not reckless. He may have a clear memory of his earlier resolve, but it no longer seems very relevant to his present condition. So he goes ahead and has more drinks. Moderating one's drinking cannot usually be achieved by making sterner resolves while in the sober state. It has to be accomplished by *training the drunken personality to be more moderate.* Ways in which this training may be done will be discussed in Chapter 12.

Rate Yourself: What Kind of Drinker Are You?

According to the latest government statistics, as published in HEW's *Second Special Report to the U.S. Congress on Alcohol and Health,* 42 percent of the adult population either does not drink or drinks only in insignificant amounts (less than once a month). Of the remainder, 31 percent are "light" drinkers who take up to 3 drinks per week, 19 percent are "moderate" drinkers taking 3 to 14 drinks per week, and 9 percent are "heavy" drinkers taking more than 14 drinks per week. This latter group is obviously a catchall, because if one divides these figures into the total U.S. alcohol consumption, one comes up with an average figure for heavy drinkers of 80 drinks a week, or slightly more than 11 per day. So let's break this category down further and we come up with the following scale:

Light drinkers take up to 3 drinks per week.

Moderate drinkers: 3 to 14 drinks per week.

Moderately heavy drinkers: 3 to 5 drinks per day.

Heavy drinkers: 6 to 12 drinks per day.

Ultra-heavy drinkers: more than 12 drinks per day.

These figures apply if you drink fairly regularly. If you're a periodic or "spree" drinker who takes his drinks all in a bunch once a week or once a month or at some other interval, then another standard of measurement applies.

Moderate spree drinkers take 3 to 5 drinks per occasion.

Heavy spree drinkers: 6 to 12 drinks.

Ultra-heavy spree drinkers: more than 12 drinks.

Effects of Excessive Drinking

Much of this will be covered in subsequent chapters, but let's summarize here what tends to happen when we drink "too much." The heavy drinker has trained his body to accept large amounts of alcohol. Since alcohol is a food, his body learns to metabolize it along with the other food it is given. This it does quite efficiently, but at some cost to itself, since alcohol contains none of the vitamins, minerals and other essential nutriments found in normal food. A deficit of these substances begins to occur. This deficit, and its accompanying discomforts, is interpreted by the drinker not as a need for better food and more vitamins, but as a need for *more alcohol.* This he proceeds to take, thereby aggravating his condition still further.

If he continues on this course, he may end up as a terminal alcoholic who has virtually abandoned food and subsists on booze alone. Along the way, he will have acquired an actual physical addiction to alcohol: he cannot stop drinking without suffering withdrawal symptoms, which may include *delirium tremens* (a hallucinatory state in which the patient shakes, trembles or moves agitatedly about while seeing or hearing bizarre sights and sounds). He will probably suffer from *alcoholic polyneuritis,* a vitamin-deficiency disease characterized by multiple aches and pains, irritability, sensory disturbances and impaired reflexes. If he persists in his drinking, he may fall into *Wernicke's syndrome,* a helpless stupor compounded by paralysis of the eyes, or *Korsakoff's psychosis,* a condition in which the memory fails and the patient becomes confused and disoriented. All these ills are due, not to alcohol, but to *nutritional deficiencies.*

2

Why Do We Drink?

THIS BOOK IS BASED in part on my own experiences with alcohol and on the experiences of about fifty other drinkers with whom I had lengthy formal interviews. In the main my informants were healthy, prosperous middle-class people, all of them moderate-to-heavy drinkers—businessmen and businesswomen, housewives, people in the professions, the arts, the media, politics, finance. Most of them were in what I would call young middle age, and had been drinking for about fifteen to twenty years. I discussed with them their drinking habits, health problems if any, social lives, sex lives, hangovers, unusual experiences with alcohol, etc. One of the questions I asked was, "What do you like about alcohol, what do you find good or helpful about it, why do you drink?"

Many of the answers were on one general theme, the theme of sociability. People drink because drinking is a friendly activity. It relaxes us, draws us closer together, helps us be lively and have fun, serves as a social solvent in gatherings that would otherwise be awkward or standoffish, helps bring the shy or inhibited individual out of his shell. There were a number of variations within the theme.

Drinking as an antidote to shyness

Many people, particularly young people, find liquor a big help in overcoming shyness or awkwardness or a feeling of being out of place. Here's how one woman put it:

I used to say liquor was my best friend because I was always shy, I could never talk to anybody. I always felt stupid and unable to speak. Then I discovered drinking when I was sixteen or seventeen, and suddenly I became like those other kids who were always talking to everybody. And then I could converse with people, join in. I was raised in such a Victorian way. I was so inhibited, still am. That's something I've had to fight all my life. I don't think I would ever have gotten out of Portland if I hadn't started drinking.

A middle-aged male:

I was very tense and ill at ease as a young man. Partly this was because of being brought up in a peculiar situation—eccentric mother, no father in the family—partly because I spent so many years in Europe. When I came back I felt out of place—not really American. It was difficult for me to feel at home or meet people or make friends. Then I began drinking, going to bars, cocktail parties. I made a lot of friends, had a succession of love affairs with girls. Actually I didn't like liquor then. It was just a means to an end—socializing, meeting people. It helped me over a difficult period, it really did. After a few drinks I was no longer afraid of people, of what they might think of me. I still drink—I do like it now—but I don't need it to feel confident.

A woman in her fifties:

I think drinking sort of quickens the mind, if you don't have too much. Then it does the reverse. I've never understood why they call it a depressant. I consider it the other thing. What's the word? Stimulant. My mind starts going a little more lively. Sometimes I think of things to say that I might be too inhibited to think of otherwise. It takes me out of my shell. I'm not afraid to join the group.

Drinking as a social solvent

Almost every one of my informants talked about how liquor promotes conviviality and good feeling, helps people "break the ice" and reach out to each other. One man said:

I associate alcohol with graciousness, the tradition of offering people something. That's why I seldom have a drink when I'm alone. I think that in any profession that requires people getting to know each other drinking is important. A long session of drinking and talking creates a bond. It's like the handshake. Shaking hands originally showed you had no weapons concealed. Drinking shows you've got nothing to hide. It's sort of a sign of trust. Without drinking I wouldn't have got to know so many people so well.

A number of people mentioned how unpleasant it is to go to parties or gatherings where no liquor is served. This is a subject on which drinkers are constantly being maligned. "If you need a drink to be sociable, that's not social drinking," says an anti-liquor pamphlet put out by the Jay Cees. Baloney! The average drinker may not be an open, spontaneously friendly person, but at least he's trying to become one. I've been to all too many gatherings of good God-fearing teetotalers where everybody sat around like sticks, once in a while interrupting the silence with remarks like "Looks like rain," or "I see by the papers that . . ." until everyone felt almost dead from boredom and embarrassment. At times like that I do wish for a drink, desperately, and I wish *they* would take one too. But when I'm in a roomful of people who are alive, friendly, trusting, vibrant, I don't miss liquor or resent their not serving it.

A public-relations man:

No way. You've *got* to have liquor when you give a press party. It loosens people up, makes them receptive. I did a couple of promotions once for a fellow who was some kind of temperance nut or something. He wouldn't let us serve booze, coffee or tea, just some stupid fruit punch. Can you imagine trying to keep a hundred press people happy on nothing but fruit punch? Hell, I couldn't keep them in the *room!* They started leaving before we even began our presentation.

Booze and the business lunch

Cartoonists make fun of the three-martini business lunch, economists complain about the millions (or is it billions?) of dollars wasted on it, the alcoholism establishment bemoans the man-hours lost because of the drunkenness of the participants, yet the business lunch goes on and on. I can't speak for any other branches of industry, but as a former magazine editor and veteran of many hundreds of "literary" lunches I can attest that their value to the publishing business is incalculable. If liquor were banned tomorrow, the whole industry would collapse.

When the lunch is with a nondrinker, particularly one who's reserved, formal or stuffy, you discuss whatever you came to discuss, make a little small talk, then pay the check and get out of the restaurant fast. Not so with the alcoholic lunch. Often the person you're meeting is a stranger or someone you only know as a voice on the telephone. But liquor makes for swift intimacy, and by the time you've had a couple of drinks you're bosom buddies, exchanging deep personal confidences and making delightfully wicked gossip about other people in the business. When you leave you feel you've made a friend for life —and sometimes you have. More important to your employer, you've made a valuable connection that will enable you to do business on a more personal and friendly basis in the future.

Liquor and the creative person

Performers and people in the arts often find that liquor helps them be more creative. I was once friendly with a night-club comic who deliberately got two-thirds drunk every night before he went out to do his act. The drunkenness helped him to ad lib and free-associate witticisms in a way he couldn't have achieved otherwise. When he wasn't working, he had no interest in liquor. I never saw him take a drink on his day off.

A couple of my interviewees mentioned using alcohol for inspiration.

Well-known jazz trumpet player:

I tend to drink occasionally when I'm playing the horn, which is when I do my heaviest drinking really. I'll have a couple of beers when I'm playing the horn. And then I'll switch to Scotch and have maybe two or three of those before the end of the evening. That gets me to a good place for playing the horn. It's not a place I would particularly enjoy if I were just at a social thing. I don't drink very much socially anymore. You tend to get fatigued toward the end of a long evening playing the horn, and drinking rests you, gives you a sense of well-being. I can see where jazz musicians who very often get bored by what they're doing, especially if they're playing the same club every night, would tend to overdrink. A lot of these guys turn into lushes, I think, just because they're trying to . . . you know, you're kind of faced with an impossible problem as a performing jazz musician where you're supposed to crank out the best you have creatively on call. Endlessly. So you turn to something else to fuel the creative instinct or turn off the pain or something, I don't know. Anyhow, it helps.

A writer:

Usually I never drink when I'm working, but once in a while I do. It's not that I'm feeling blocked or discouraged or anything. It's —I don't know, perhaps I feel I'm too self-critical. I've done some rather surprising things when practically dead drunk—surprising to me, anyway. Of course they need a lot of editing. And I feel ghastly the next day.

Drinking as a consciousness alterer

Several of my informants said they liked drinking because it puts them into an alternate state of mind or consciousness. One of them said:

It's like going to another country. It's one way of . . . traveling without leaving, physically. It's closely related too, I think, to music. It gives you some sort of release. Also I like it, the social ambience of it. I like a bar scene which is impersonal and yet there is some sociability there. You meet people and feel good. It's a non-traumatic experience. Whereas, you know, jobs and so many other things are.

And another:

> Liquor was a revelation to me at first. It's like—well, I don't know, it's hard to explain. It's like here I was this punk kid in a small town and I'd been brought up in a certain way, you know, and I thought, this is it, this is the way I am, this is the way my folks are, and it's never going to change. Then suddenly I get all drunk and start stumbling and falling down—all that stuff—puking, and laughing and crying. . . . It was like, Hey, man! anything can happen. Look at me, I'm drunk! It kind of changed my view of things, made me think if I can be this, why, hell, I can be anything.

How drinkers really feel about liquor

Many drinkers act as if they think drinking is a hilarious, often ridiculous pastime. They kid each other about how drunk they get, tell stories about how so-and-so passed out in a poison-ivy patch or went in swimming with all his clothes on, and so forth. In my interviews, however, I asked rather serious questions and got serious answers in return. A surprising number of people revealed rather deep feelings about liquor and drinking. Drinking has a value to them which they never discuss ordinarily, perhaps because it is too important, too basic.

I think that most, perhaps all, drinkers drink as a life-affirming act—a quest for love, a reaching-out toward one's fellow man, a search for one's own better nature and for the mysteries of life. *That* is the secret the barroom banter tries to conceal.

3

Demon Rum:
Public Opinion and the
Politics of Alcohol

Let us take a look . . . at the so-called drink problem, a small
subdivision of the larger problem of saving men from their
inherent and incurable hoggishness. What is the salient feature of
the discussion of the drink problem, as one observes it going on
eternally in These States? The salient feature is that very few
honest and intelligent men ever take a hand in the business. . . .
On the one hand, it is labored by a horde of obvious jackasses,
each confident that he can dispose of it overnight. And on the
other hand it is sophisticated and obscured by a crowd of oblique
fellows, hired by interested parties, whose secret desire is that it be
kept unsolved. . . . Why does one hear so little about it from
those who have no personal stake in it, and can thus view it fairly
and accurately?

—H. L. Mencken, *Prejudices*

TO UNDERSTAND present-day American attitudes toward
drinking and drinkers, one needs to know a little about the
history of this century. For most rural and small-town Americans, liquor was evil and drinking a sin. Sherwood Anderson
tells of seeing in his boyhood the saloonkeeper who lived on his
street walk by silently with bent head. The man's wife and child

seldom ventured out of their house. "It was an age of temperance societies and there were two churches on our street. To sell liquor, to own a saloon, was to be, I am sure, the devil's servant."

The "drys" felt that they were engaged in a holy crusade. Any lie that they propagated about liquor was therefore a pious one, any distortion of scientific or medical facts a commendable presentation. Alcohol was represented as the prime cause of crime, sexual aberration, epilepsy, feeble-mindedness, venereal disease and racial degeneration. Alcohol was said to poison fetuses in the womb, and parents who drank were called murderers of unborn babies. According to Andrew Sinclair in *Era of Excess,* a ". . . favorite trick of temperance lecturers was to drop the contents of an egg into a glass of pure alcohol and tell their audiences that the curdled mass was similar to the effect of liquor on the lining of the human stomach. A similar horror technique was the threat . . . that drunkards might suddenly catch fire and burn to death, breathing out blue flame. The idea that children born in drunkenness would be defective was stressed and documented."

A best-selling health manual, *Dr. Gunn's New Family Physician,* had this to say about drink:

> Intemperance not only destroys the health, but inflicts ruin upon the innocent and helpless, for it invades the family and social circle and spreads woe and sorrow all around; it cuts down youth in all its vigor, manhood in its strength, and age in its weakness; it breaks the father's heart, bereaves the doting mother, extinguishes natural affection, erases conjugal love, blots out filial attachment, blights parental hope, and brings down mourning age in sorrow to the grave. It produces fevers, feeds rheumatism, nurses the gout, welcomes epidemics, invites disease, imparts pestilence, embraces consumption, cherishes dyspepsia, and encourages apoplexy and paralytic affections. . . . Let no man keep company with his wife for the sake of posterity, except when he is sober, for children usually prove wine-bibbers and drunkards whose parents begat them when drunk.

Organizations such as the Anti-Saloon League hired famous orators to give anti-liquor speeches. One famous speaker, Richmond Pearson Hobson, earned over $170,000 in nine years (equivalent to over a million in today's money) giving patriotic, anti-alcohol lectures, in which he made statements like this:

> As young as our Nation is, the deadly work of alcohol has already blighted liberty in our greatest cities. At the present rate of the growth of cities over country life, if no check is put upon the spread of alcoholic degeneracy, the day cannot be far distant when liberty in great States must go under.

Another famous and highly-paid orator, William Jennings Bryan, composed veritable prose poems of "dry" sentiment:

> Water, the daily need of every living thing. It ascends from the seas, obedient to the summons of the sun, and, descending, showers blessing upon the earth; it gives of its sparkling beauty to the fragrant flower; its alchemy transmutes base clay into golden grain; it is the canvas upon which the finger of the Infinite traces the radiant bow of promise. It is the drink that refreshes and adds no sorrow with it—Jehovah looked upon it at creation's dawn and said —"It is good."

With the coming of World War I, prohibitionists could add extra fervor to the patriotic motif and urge legislators "to abolish the un-American, pro-German, crime-producing, food-wasting, youth-corrupting, home-wrecking, treasonable liquor traffic."

Doctors and pharmacists were responsive to anti-alcohol pressure. In 1916, *The Pharmacopoeia of the United States* deleted whiskey and brandy from its list of standard drugs. A year later, the House of Delegates of the American Medical Association passed a resolution stating that the AMA opposed the use of alcohol as a beverage; believed there was no scientific basis for its use in therapeutics or as a tonic, stimulant or food; and that the use of alcohol as a therapeutic agent should be discouraged—this despite the fact that in those years a huge majority of the members of the AMA did indeed prescribe alcohol as a therapeutic agent for a wide variety of complaints, and would continue to do so.

As Andrew Sinclair says in *Era of Excess:*

> The resolution was extremely useful to the drys in their campaign for national prohibition. Senator Sterling, of South Dakota, referred to it in the debate on the Eighteenth Amendment as "one of the most valuable pieces of evidence we can find in support of the submission of this amendment to the several States of the Union." Wayne B. Wheeler quoted it as definitive evidence while defending the dry definition of "intoxicating" in the courts. The resolution was also very profitable to the doctors. After the passage of the Eighteenth Amendment and the Volstead Act, they were the only people who could issue to their patients whiskey, brandy and other strong drinks. Moreover, no patent medicine containing alcohol could be officially sold without a doctor's prescription. By constitutional amendment, the doctors controlled all supplies of beverage alcohol in the United States, except for the hard cider of the farmers and the sacramental wine of the priests.

(How profitable? In one year of prohibition, 1928, it was estimated that the doctors of America earned about $40 million by writing prescriptions for whiskey.)

In 1919, the Eighteenth Amendment, prohibiting the manufacture or sale of alcoholic beverages (except for therapeutic or sacramental purposes) was added to the Constitution. That the amendment did not succeed in eliminating Demon Rum was a great disappointment to most drys, driving some of them to frenzies of hatred toward drinkers. In *Era of Excess,* Sinclair quotes answers to a prize competition for better ways of enforcing prohibition:

> One woman suggested that liquor law violators should be hung by the tongue beneath an airplane and carried over the United States. Another suggested that the government should distribute poison liquor through the bootleggers; she admitted that several hundred thousand Americans would die, but she thought this cost was worth the proper enforcement of the dry law. Others wanted

to deport all aliens, exclude wets from all churches, force bootleggers to go to church every Sunday, forbid drinkers to marry, torture or whip or brand or sterilize or tattoo drinkers, place offenders in bottle-shaped cages in public squares, make them swallow two ounces of castor oil, and even execute the consumers of alcohol and their posterity to the fourth generation.

America reacts to prohibition

In winning the battle of prohibition, it turned out, the dry forces lost their war—a war to assert the virtues of the countryside over the vices of the city, the righteousness of the native American over the dissolute ways of foreigners and immigrants. Prohibition made drinking glamorous. Where it had been a vice of the working class, drinking now became a badge of sophistication, a mark of wealth and savoir-faire. To take a drink was to strike a blow against repression and to assert one's superiority over the repressive, know-nothing class H. L. Mencken had christened "the booboisie." Middle-class people who had never before had any interest in drinking hastened to find themselves bootleggers and get introductions to speakeasies. Women, too, began to drink as never before, to the point where, as Heywood Broun commented, a man had to fight his way through crowds of schoolgirls to make his way to the bar.

It was not just drinking that became popular. Urban America became infatuated with almost *everything* the drys disapproved of: dancing, cigarette smoking, card playing, even (among the more daring souls) the smoking of opium and sniffing of cocaine. This was the age of the Flapper, who smoked, drank, danced the tango and Charleston. Virtually all the celebrities and "opinion leaders" of the 1920s were wets. Jimmy Walker, with his penchant for chorus girls and "black velvets" (champagne laced with Guinness stout) became mayor of New York. Authors like John O'Hara and F. Scott Fitzgerald celebrated the hard-drinking ways of the "Jazz Age."

Drunkenness was a badge of manliness for men, of emancipation for women. Almost everybody who was anybody drank. Think of John Barrymore, Sinclair Lewis, Dorothy Parker, Gene Fowler, Wilson Mizner, W. C. Fields . . . Fields's attitudes about liquor were a low-comedy exaggeration of wet opinion. As Robert Lewis Taylor tells the story in *W. C. Fields, His Follies and Fortunes:*

Grady was driving the car through the South one night while Fields sat in the back seat on the trunk. The comedian was drinking what he described as "martinis"; he had a bottle of gin in one hand and a bottle of vermouth in the other, and he took alternate pulls, favoring the gin. At an intersection in a country town they saw a man with a satchel making signals under a street lamp. Grady said, "Fellow wants a ride."

"Pick him up," cried Fields. "Where's your sense of charity?"

Grady slowed down, called out, "Hop in the back," and waited till the man got aboard. As they drove off, Fields extended the bottle of gin to him, but the man refused with a look of offended piety. About five miles down the road, the stranger took some tracts out of his coat pocket and said, "Brothers, I'm a minister of the gospel."

Fields blew a mouthful of gin on the floor and the man went on, "You're sinning in this automobile and though I don't ordinarily do no free preaching, I'm going to preach a free sermon right here. He examined the tracts and added, "To tell you the truth, I'm a-going to give you Number Four."

"What's Number Four?" said Fields.

"Called the 'Evils of Alcohol,' " said the minister.

Fields leaned over and said to Grady, "Pull up beside the first ditch you see."

The minister's narrative had reached a point where a roustabout had pawned his small daughter's shoes to raise money for a drink when Grady slammed on the brakes.

"*Aus! Aus!*" Fields began to cry, harking back to his German period, and he kicked the minister into the ditch. Then he opened his trunk, removed an unopened bottle of gin, and tossed it down beside him. "There's my Number Three," he yelled. "Called 'How to Keep Warm in a Ditch.' "

Grady drove on. Fields told him afterward he'd suspected the minister might be a Methodist. He'd had a lot of trouble with Methodists, he said.

If prohibition was bulldozed into law by propaganda tactics that prefigured those of Hitler, Stalin and Mao Tse-tung, repeal was brought about, in part, by an even more potent weapon—laughter and ridicule. How could one forever retain a statute that had become a joke? So in 1933, a year of deep Depression, the Twenty-first Amendment superseded the Eighteenth. The newsreels of the day showed great merriment on the occasion, with crowds toasting the cameras in bars, taverns and cocktail lounges (the word "saloon," in deference to the drys, had been made taboo and still remains so). But with the Depression and its attendant unemployment, the nation was anything but merry.

The medical profession makes its move

In 1935, the American Medical Association, which had been rather quiescent during prohibition, passed another resolution, displaying again the acute sense of timing and of enlightened self-interest which it had possessed for so long (until recently; in the last two decades it has begun to offend its own members by being too conservative and power-hungry). Rather mildly, the AMA declared that alcoholics were valid patients for a physician. This shot would, later on, be heard around the nation.

In the beginning of the century, the medical profession had made an unsuccessful try to achieve control over intoxication by forming an organization known as The American Association for the Study of Inebriety and Narcotics, whose official publication was the *Journal of Inebriety.* This move had gone virtually unnoticed, even among physicians, amid the avalanches of dry propaganda—and possibly the word "inebriety" was one that did not appeal to the public. Furthermore, half of the goals of the association had been made useless, in 1914, by the passage of the Harrison Narcotic Act, controlling the sale and distribution of opium and opium derivatives. Doctors could claim little credit for the Harrison Act—it was passed partly as a lagniappe to the dry movement (which was against *all* intoxicants), partly in deference to the rather strong anti-Chinese sentiment in the country. But after repeal, an *éminence grise* of the alcoholism establishment, Dr. E. M. Jellinek, reports:

> While the work of the old Society and its slogan "inebriety is a disease" was practically forgotten in America, it remained alive in Europe, although not prominently, and it floated back to America to be developed and elaborated here by psychiatrists. This psychiatric work gave a new impetus to physiopathologists for turning from the study of peripheral problems to research on the etiology of "alcoholism." This trend gave rise to vigorous polemics between psychiatrists on the one side and physiopathologists and pharmacologists on the other side, but the controversy brought and continues to bring clarification, even though at times it engenders some confusion.
>
> The conception of alcoholism as a disease became not only a working hypothesis in research and in the clinical treatment of some varieties of alcoholism but also the central point of certain community activities related to the problem of alcohol. The "renewed" idea found its way not only into professional circles but far into public opinion, until now in America one may speak of a majority acceptance of the illness conception of "alcoholism."
>
> That the "new approach" has penetrated public opinion rapidly may be ascribed to a number of organizations devoted to research or education or rehabilitation or all three. The greatest roles were played in this process by the "Yale group," the Research Council on Problems of Alcohol (now defunct); the National Council on Alcoholism (formerly National Committee for Education on Alcoholism) and its local affiliates; the Committee on Alcoholism of the American Medical Association; the state government agencies in charge of "alcoholism programs"; and last but not least, that large group of men and women who would not like to be called an organization, namely the fellowship of Alcoholics Anonymous.

With the collapse of evangelical Christianity's hold on the media, after the prohibition debacle, a defeat accentuated by the irreverent counterattack of the wets, a spiritual vacuum began to exist in the United States. There was no generally recognized authority which could pass on moral or social dilemmas. This gap the medical profession proceeded to fill. In fairness, no takeover conspiracies existed. Despite a certain readiness, the medical profession did not invite the takeover—it was drafted. One might call physicians the reluctant priesthood. Throughout the thirties the public became gradually more infatuated with the doctor-as-hero. Movies like the Doctor Kildare series were being turned out by every major studio. Books and novels about medical men were bestsellers. Magazines like the *Reader's Digest* found the profession good copy and turned out hundreds of articles on medical topics. With the help of the AMA's superb public-relations machine, the mystique of the physician as superbeing—kindly, wise and all-knowing, bound to a strict humanitarian code of ethics through his quasi-religious Hippocratic Oath—was widely propagated.

At the same time, the profession was expanding its powers, claiming dominion over vast new territories—mental illness, alcoholism, drug addiction, the control of obesity. The AMA was winning its battle with its long-time enemy, the patent-medicine industry—many proprietary medicines were taken off the market, others restricted to sale by prescription only, and the manufacturers of the remaining products, in many cases, were forced to include a "commercial" to the medical profession on every package ("If symptoms persist, consult your physician," etc.).

The readiness of the profession to serve as an agent of social control was welcomed by government. What a neat solution to the problem of handling deviant citizens—drunken, disorderly, eccentric or obstreperous persons—define them as "ill" and turn them over to the doctors for "treatment"! That the treatment in many cases has been ineffective is of little importance; government has found it handy to co-opt the medical profession and give it powers over various social problems. Today's physician is an important functionary with much authority over the public at large. He can give them or deny them access to drugs and medication, certify them as insane, alcoholic or drug-addicted, even decide whether to keep them alive or let them die. There is a good deal of truth in the contention of Dr. Thomas Szasz (author of *Ceremonial Chemistry, The Myth of Mental Illness,* and other books critical of medical orthodoxy) that we are now living in a "pharmacratic" society.

While some doctors welcome their new powers and responsibilities, others resent them as an imposition, because as it gave the doctors more power, government also asserted more control over them. It tells them which modes of treatment they may use and which not, which drugs they may prescribe (and in what dosage) and which not.

The "official" view of alcohol

Like any priesthood, the medical profession is highly sensitive to public opinion. Like the religious priest who preaches "thou shalt not kill" in time of peace, then in time of war calls on the Lord to smite our enemies, medical priests hasten to comply with public sentiment—by removing out-of-favor drugs (amphetamines, barbiturates) from their armamentariums, for instance.

The medical view of alcohol, which is the official one today, attempts to reconcile the broadest possible spectrum of both "wet" and "dry" sentiment. Alcohol is no longer considered evil, but is now a "medically suspect" substance. "Responsible" (moderate) drinking is condoned or even given mild approval while "irresponsible" drinking, which leads to illness or is in itself an illness, is deplored. The irresponsible drinker himself is not to blame, however: he is suffering from an illness that compels him to drink. This kind of medical theology can sometimes seem as foolish as earlier theologies which argued over how many angels can dance on the point of a pin. Dr. Szasz quotes from an editorial in *The American Journal of Psychiatry* which noted approvingly that the "public image" of the alcoholic has been changed successfully from that of a "skid-row derelict to that of a worthwhile person suffering from an illness which can be successfully arrested so that he (or she) can take his rightful place in society—a good parent, good spouse, good neighbor, good worker, and a productive citizen with a social conscience." Dr. Szasz goes on to comment:

> I doubt that any leading medical journal would assert, in equally sweeping terms, that patients suffering from diabetes, hypertension, or tuberculosis, are, one and all, "worthwhile persons." What, I should like to know, makes the alcoholic—*any* alcoholic, according to the quotation cited—a "worthwhile person"? If alcoholism is a disease, like other diseases, how can it impart moral value to the person who has it? If having a disease does not make an individual worthless, it also cannot make him worthwhile! To my mind, an individual is a worthwhile or worthless human being—depending on what he does or does not do with his life—whether he has diabetes, heart trouble, or the habit of drinking too much.
>
> If alcoholism is a disease, why do we need propagandists and politicians to tell us so? We neither need nor use laymen to tell us that cancer and heart disease are illnesses. Why, then, do we need President Johnson to proclaim that "The alcoholic suffers from a disease which will yield eventually to scientific research and adequate treatment."?

Myth or not (we'll examine that question in a subsequent chapter), the idea that "irresponsible" drinking is an illness called alcoholism is an integral part of the official view of alcohol. The main keeper and unfolder of this view is an organization called the National Institute on Alcohol Abuse and Alcoholism, which is part of the U.S. Department of Health, Education and Welfare. Their latest report, issued in June, 1974, is a curious mixture of polls, surveys, statistics, medical scholarship and propaganda. In his introduction, the director of the institute, Dr. Morris E. Chafetz, declares: "As an illness, alcoholism is devastating; the source of accidents and poor health; a contributor to the disruption of families; a well of human misery. Something is being done about it."

Part of what is being done is to propagandize against alcohol. Through its "educational" arm, the institute releases many pamphlets and other materials—also those TV commercials depicting the evils of drink in which the announcer says at the end something like, "If you want to help write 'Alcohol,' Rockville, Maryland." These activities are bearing fruit, the 1974 report notes. It quotes from a survey of American attitudes toward alcohol showing increasing "public awareness" of alcoholism between 1971, shortly after the institute was founded, and 1973. This awareness is shown by increasing approval of a number of statements:

Statement	% Approving 1971	% Approving 1973	Change
Heavy drinking is a very serious problem in the country today	59	72	+22%
Alcohol is a drug	61	72	+18%
There is no known cure for a hangover	45	50	+11%
Drunkenness is usually like an overdose of drugs	31	43	+39%
A host who encourages heavy drinking among his guests can be described as a			
—drug pusher	19	33	+74%
—bad host	50	58	+15%

The report also has a section on the "Economic Costs of Alcohol-Related Problems" in which it estimates that the nation loses $25 billion every year owing to alcohol-related absenteeism and loss of production, accidents, medical costs, criminal and welfare system costs, and so on. "Related" is a favorite term of the medico-governmental theologians when talking about condemned or suspect substances—an abundance of statistics has also been published on "drug-related" crime, absenteeism, etc. (If television ever comes under attack, we'll probably be provided with statistics on "television-related" crime, absenteeism, etc. One remembers how hundreds of comic books were hounded off the newsstands in the 1950s after psychiatrist Dr. Fredric Wertham published an article asserting that the comics were psychologically damaging to children.)

Although the alcoholism establishment has many intelligent, talented scientists among its members, it is hampered in its quest for the truth about alcohol by a need to demonstrate large-scale ravages. Multi-million-dollar budgets cannot be maintained and augmented unless the need for such budgets can be demonstrated. Thus there is a tendency to define alcoholism in the broadest possible terms, so that as large as possible a segment of the population can be shown to be alcoholic. The figure currently mentioned for the number of alcoholics in the United States is 9 million. By a curious coincidence, 9 million is also the number of Americans estimated by the 1974 institute report to be heavy drinkers. In other words, *all* heavy drinkers are counted as alcoholics!

A Nobel prizewinner once remarked that if a cure for cancer were discovered tomorrow the discovery would not be cause for unmitigated joy in the cancer-research community. His remark would seem even more applicable to alcohol research. The alcoholism establishment has an incurable "Yes, but" attitude toward hopeful-seeming discoveries. It did not cheer when Roger Williams and other workers demonstrated that many alcoholic symptoms were produced by nutritional deficiencies and might be relieved by vitamins. On the contrary, it redoubled its effort to prove that alcohol *in itself* is a harmful substance. The most widely-hailed alcohol experiment in recent years was one by Drs. Emanuel Rubin and Charles S. Lieber employing thirty-two baboons. The baboons were divided into two groups of sixteen, a control group and an experimental group. All were fed an adequate diet plus "more vitamins and minerals than the recommended amount for the baboon," but the experimental subjects were given alcohol to the extent of 50 percent of their total calories. All of the alcohol-fed animals developed fatty livers, five of them alcoholic hepatitis and two cirrhosis of the liver. This was a breakthrough—the first time in over sixty years of experimentation that anyone had been able to induce cirrhosis in an animal through the use of alcohol!

Although many meticulously-performed experiments have come out of the alcohol-research movement, one can criticize it on the whole for:

1. Exaggerating its constituency and thus not pinpointing those persons most in need of medical help.

2. Concentrating its experiments, whether through funding practices or the personal interests of participating scientists, on studies calculated to demonstrate the noxious effects of alcohol.

3. Failing to pursue promising lines of inquiry or do follow-up research on studies that might prove helpful to the drinking population. Why has nobody done a follow-up study on pyritinol, for instance? (See Chapter 7, "The Hangover.")

Role of the liquor industry

Although it maintains a large public-relations operation (Distilled Spirits Council of the United States or DISCUS, formerly known as Licensed Beverage Industries) the liquor industry has been keeping a very low profile. It is possibly the only industry that rejects and disavows its own best customers. Obviously alcoholics and heavy drinkers account for a huge percentage of liquor sales, but you'd never know it from liquor ads, which invariably depict the product being served in respectable if not glamorous upper-class settings, nor from the public-information pamphlets put out by DISCUS, which include such topics as *If You Choose to Drink, Drink Responsibly* and . . . *To Your Health.* The liquor industry has embraced the alcoholism-as-disease concept with enthusiasm. In . . . *To Your Health* there is a quotation from an article in the AMA publication *Today's Health:*

> It is unreasonable to stop the manufacture and sale of alcoholic beverages because a comparative few are harmed by them. The prohibitionist approach penalized the majority because some people reacted abnormally to alcohol. It can be compared to prohibiting the sale of sugar because our diabetic population would be harmed by its excessive use. It was obvious that the problem of alcoholism rests in the one who uses it, not in the beverage.

The industry co-sponsors and participates in many organizations such as the National Council on Alcoholism, the Alcohol and Drug Problems Association of North America and the International Council on Alcohol and Addictions, and has helped fund a number of research projects, conferences and training programs. Thus it now has a voice in the major organizations devoted to the study, control and rehabilitation of alcoholics.

The practicing physician

The average doctor in private practice is an overworked individual who spends most of his waking hours tending to patients and has little time to do any independent research or investigation. For information on new drugs and methods of treatment he depends largely on the medical journals and on information supplied by the drug companies through their salesmen or "detailers." Though some physicians cling to older views of illness and treatment methods, most doctors try to keep up-to-date, and the up-to-date information they're getting on alcohol is of course the "official" view. In researching this book, I was surprised to find that what I thought would be easiest to come by —a GP or internist who would talk to me at length about the health problems of drinkers—was in fact difficult. The profession has a tendency to lump all drinkers into two groups—moderate ("responsible") drinkers, who have few health problems, and "alcoholics" ("irresponsible" drinkers), who ought to stop. "I can't help you. I don't do much with alcoholics" was a response I heard frequently. Or "I tell them to cut down on their drinking, or join AA." The general feeling seems to be that it's best to try to eliminate the primary "illness"—whether it be called alcoholism, problem drinking or simply heavy drinking —than to try to prevent "side effects" (though these of course are treated when clinically apparent).

I found anti-alcohol sentiment quite pronounced among most of the doctors I spoke to, even those who in their off hours drink quite freely themselves. The psychiatrists were even more negative. I had hoped to find a psychiatrist or two who might feel that drinking had at least some aspects that were psychologically beneficial (as did Freud, for instance), but after asking about twelve of them, "Do you have anything *good* to say about drinking?" and getting twelve "Nos" I gave up the search.

Although America is now wet, that self-designated nanny of all drinkers, the alcoholism establishment, is glaring down at us with an awfully dry eye.

4

What's Good About Alcohol? Some Medical Views

ALCOHOL IN MODERATE AMOUNTS cheers people up, promotes conviviality and has many beneficial effects on the human organism. The best illustration of the helpful aspects of alcohol is that moderate drinkers live longer than teetotalers. Dr. Morris E. Chafetz, Director of the National Institute of Alcohol Abuse and Alcoholism, says that moderate drinking seems to increase longevity and reduce the odds of developing heart disease. Moderate drinkers, he says, live longer and have a lower rate of reported heart attacks than ex-drinkers or abstainers. One of the most comprehensive demonstrations of this fact was made by biostatistician Dr. Raymond Pearl of Johns Hopkins. Dr. Pearl made a long-range study of ninety-four pairs of siblings. One brother in each pair was a teetotaler, the other a drinker. The study showed that the drinkers lived longer than the nondrinkers. In fact, the study had to be abandoned when the last of the nondrinking brothers died.

Alcohol has many uses in medicine, but it has been somewhat out of fashion of late years. In Europe wine is prescribed for a wide variety of ailments, for instance, but in this country we're more inclined to the latest miracle drug, whatever it may be.

Suppose alcohol had never existed, but a new drug with the same properties as alcohol had just been invented? Dr. William Dock once speculated on this theme, giving the new substance the fictitious name of "Methyl Methanol":

> Let us suppose that methylmethanol, a substance recently synthesized, was found to be completely free of the ill effects, allergic reactions, blood cell damage, and the other hazards associated with nearly all our antibiotics and sedatives. But methylmethanol, in small doses, proved to be a superb tranquilizer; in larger doses, a good sedative; and in even larger doses, an effective anesthetic agent. Small doses even improved the ability to solve certain kinds of difficult problems in the calculus. In addition, it dilated blood vessels, caused a decrease in the production of the pituitary antidiuretic hormone, and could be used as a readily absorbed body fuel, up to one third the daily need for calories. It also increased the absorption of fats in patients with intestinal malabsorption and gave better appetites to many sick people.
>
> We all know what would happen. The sales of all other sedatives and tranquilizers would slump, four-page spreads in medical journals, and neat stories in the papers and news weeklies would make M-M a household name like aspirin and milltown. The stock of the patent licensees would go through the ceiling on Wall Street. The lucky discoverer would get every possible honor, as did the men who gave us insulin and hay fever pills. The medical school where the studies were made would found an institute supported by millions in royalties. Humanity would be benefited for untold thousands of years, and the Russians would announce that they had discovered M-M back in Czar Nicholas's day.

Alcohol produces its maximum benefits when used as a food, that is, as part of a regular meal in not very large amounts. When you take a glass or two of wine or a bottle of beer with your meal, the alcohol contributes to the metabolism much as do fats or carbohydrates, "sparing" the proteins—that is, leaving the proteins to build body tissue and using the alcohol along with fat and carbohydrates to produce energy. Also, the psychological effect of the alcohol, acting as it does as both a mild tranquilizer and euphoriant, helps produce a feeling of well-being. For centuries, alcohol was prescribed routinely as a tonic, and it does have many tonic effects on the body.

Appetite stimulation

A small amount of alcohol, one drink or two, acts to enhance the appetite, especially if the drink contains very little sugar and at least some bitter or sour-tasting constituents. A true aperitif should not contain more than 20 percent alcohol. Such wines as sherry or vermouth, or aperitifs like Dubonnet or Campari, are excellent appetite inducers. With a mixed drink made with hard liquor there should be considerable dilution of the liquor. In other words, a martini or a manhattan is not quite as appetite stimulating as something weaker. The stimulating effect from your drink occurs instantaneously, but does not last very long, perhaps twenty minutes. If you want to have maximum appetite, then, you should eat fairly soon after drinking and drink no more than two glasses of wine or two fairly weak cocktails. If you keep on drinking the appetite-enhancing effect disappears.

In some cases adding alcohol to the diet of people who are weak, rundown or convalescent is often dramatically useful. For instance: a patient recovering from a long, serious illness is uncomfortable, apprehensive, doesn't rest well, and has no appetite. He has lost weight during his ordeal and needs to be built up. He does not seem to absorb sufficient nourishment from his regular diet. In addition to this he's cranky and needs sedation every night. Now, if you add generous amounts of alcohol to his diet you produce a very different picture. From the alcohol the patient is getting a readily available source of calories, which enable him to better utilize the proteins in his diet toward rebuilding his depleted organism. The alcohol makes him more cheerful, more relaxed, and chances are he will no longer need to take a sleeping pill before he gets to sleep. He will begin to gain weight. He'll have a better appetite—in short, what might have been a long, drawn-out convalescence is much speeded up.

People who don't digest well because they don't produce enough gastric acid can be markedly helped by alcohol, particularly if it's in the form of table wine. Both red and white table wine also contain significant amounts of iron, most of which is in the reduced or ferrous form, which is readily absorbed by the organism. The patient with iron-deficiency anemia who drinks three glasses of table wine per day will get 25 percent or more of his daily iron requirement, which is why wine has been prescribed for anemia for a century or more.

Alcohol, the heart and the arteries

There is evidence that alcohol acts in ways not yet completely known to prevent disease in the coronary arteries and cardiovascular disease. Researchers have repeatedly found that coronary disease is significantly less frequent in countries where wine is part of the everyday diet. Whether or not it is actually a preventive, alcohol is certainly extremely useful in cases where disease involving the heart or arteries does exist. It acts to dilate the peripheral blood vessels, thus reducing the load on the heart, and in addition soothes the tensions and anxieties which usually come along with these ailments. Heart specialists have recognized the value of alcohol for over two centuries. For generations, alcohol was the recognized drug for angina pectoris, for instance, and is still considered by many doctors equal, and for some cases superior, to the nitrate treatment. The famous cardiologist Paul Dudley White recommended alcohol to many of his patients. Another cardiologist, Irving S. Wright, former president of the American Heart Association, prescribes an ounce or two of whiskey every four hours for patients with arteriosclerosis, adding, "Few, if any, drugs for dilating the arteries are as effective." Angina is an acute and extremely painful spasm caused by clogged (sclerosed) coronary arteries. When an attack occurs, an ounce or two of distilled spirits often gives relief from the pain, usually in only a few minutes. For this purpose, straight whiskey or some undiluted spirit should be taken because what is needed is the rapid absorption of the alcohol. It has been shown that alcohol is also useful in preventing anginal attacks by helping the patient keep some measure of vasodilation. In these cases, any form of alcohol, including wine and beer, can be used. Distilled spirits are also sometimes prescribed for anginal patients to be taken before any extraordinary effort or excitement in order to prevent an attack.

Alcohol is useful, too, in treating high blood pressure. A small amount of whiskey or brandy will lower the blood pressure considerably and keep it lower for three or four hours before it rises to its previous level.

Diabetes

The diabetic, who has to reduce drastically his intake of sugars and carbohydrates, can be particularly benefited by alcohol. As Chauncey Leake says in his book *Alcoholic Beverages in Clinical Medicine,*

> Long before the introduction of insulin in diabetes therapy, and even after insulin became available, alcoholic beverages were customarily prescribed for diabetic patients. Many European clinicians still regularly employed them, dry table wines in particular, as an important part of the diabetic diet, for the physiological as well as the psychological well-being of the subject. In the United States, the use of alcoholic beverages in diabetic therapy fell into temporary disfavor during Prohibition, but, according to Lucia and others, many American physicians have returned to the use of appropriate alcoholic beverages in uncomplicated diabetes with generally satisfactory results. Joslin has reported that in no disease is the employment of alcohol more useful or more justifiable.

Unfortunately, there are quite a few doctors in this country who still have the prohibition spirit and who advise their diabetic patients to refrain from drinking although there is absolutely no clinical reason for this advice. Studies have shown that the diabetic can drink as much as twenty-four ounces of dry table wine daily with no significant rise in his blood-sugar levels. Psychologically, the freedom to drink can be extremely important for a diabetic because of his restricted and often unpleasurable diet. With severe diabetics, many doctors try to forbid alcohol because they're afraid the patient will lose track of time while drinking and forget to take his insulin shots.

A complication of diabetes is arteriosclerosis. Here again, the vasodilating effect of alcohol can be quite helpful. Cholesterol buildup in the diabetic is much more rapid than in the normal individual. As Walton Hall Smith and Ferdinand C. Helwig, M.D. state in their book, *Liquor, the Servant of Man:*

> . . . arteriosclerosis [is] the disease which, if accompanied by diabetes, makes young men old half a generation too soon. From the poorly converted fat, down into the intima of the arteries, is laid away the cholesterol which causes it. This we know. And insulin doesn't stop it but will permit the reverse. This too is known. We do not know precisely what alcohol does to the cholesterol; we only know that in the presence of alcohol much of it seems to disappear as though dissolved; that arteriosclerosis in habitual drinkers is reduced in striking percentage.

The ultimate disease

This disease is incurable, and inevitable. It is old age. Its main symptoms are hardening of the arteries, faulty digestion, insomnia, emotional depression. I have a relative who is suffering from it. Occasionally he comes for dinner in the evening. I find him full of entertainment and charm in his reminiscences and good humor. At my house his circulation is good, and so are his appetite, digestion, and mood, and he goes home and gets a good sleep. He accomplishes this on one highball before dinner and one toddy before leaving. His daughter, with whom he is unlucky enough to reside, often remarks how well he seems after being out. She says it does him good to get out and I agree with her. She won't permit him to "take anything" in her house because she doesn't want him to get dependent upon it. She doesn't want him to get the habit. He is 83 years old.

(Smith and Helwig, *Liquor, The Servant of Man*)

Many elderly people tend to be cranky and irritable, or morose and depressed, or withdrawn and despondent. Physicians in charge of nursing homes and homes for the elderly have been finding in recent years that they can prescribe a drink or two rather than the multitude of tranquilizers, mood elevators and sedatives which they formerly employed. In many nursing homes, introducing a cocktail hour has resulted in a dramatic improvement in the general atmosphere. The place begins to seem more like a home than a hospital, the patients become more gregarious and cheerful, and more civilized and sociable. Introducing liquor gives the patients more dignity and makes them seem more like senior adults than elderly children at the mercy of attendants and doctors. At the Ann Lee Home and Infirmary in Albany, New York, for instance, Dr. George A. Cuttita found that when he began serving nightly drinks of brandy to his patients, the number of patients taking tranquilizers dropped from 40 percent to only 18 percent.

5

Alcohol, Nutrition and Your Health

I . . . herewith positively assert that *no one who follows good nutritional practices will ever become an alcoholic.* This is obvious, when you think of it. It usually requires seven to ten years of heavy drinking to produce an alcoholic, and during the time of heavy drinking, the alcoholic to be is violating the most basic rules of good nutrition by ingesting far too large a proportion of his energy in the form of naked calories.

Dr. Roger J. Williams, *Nutrition Against Disease*

When there is a high alcoholic intake or even often in so-called social drinking a high intake of vitamins is especially desirable because of the extensive often-hidden damage done by alcohol. A greater intake of vitamins is necessary because vitamins B_1, B_6 and biotin are necessary to support the oxidation-inducing enzymes; nicotinic acid and B_2 are needed to overcome the inhibition of metabolic conversions caused by alcohol; vitamin E to prevent the increased peroxidation of fats in the liver; more folic acid, vitamins B_6 and B_{12} to repair the tissue damage that alcohol produces; and vitamin C to keep connective tissue in healthy condition. The whole principle is one of *repair* and *replacement*—the repair of tissues (when possible) and the replacement of the vitamins either excreted or not taken in food. Increased urination during drinking also can deplete minerals which should be replaced through food.

Dr. Erwin Di Cyan, *Vitamins in Your Life*

ADEQUATE NUTRITION is important to anyone who drinks and vital to anyone who drinks at all heavily. Virtually *all* the ills that drinkers are subject to come not from drinking itself but from the accompanying nutritional deficiencies. Perhaps alcohol does cause some direct cellular damage—some recent experiments have suggested the possibility—but this fact has never been proven. What has been amply demonstrated is that protein, vitamin and mineral deficiencies due to drinking are commonplace, even among moderate social drinkers.

Even when someone adheres to a diet that would normally be adequate, if he adds liquor to the diet he will begin to suffer deficiencies. Dr. Norman Jolliffe, of the New York University–Bellevue Medical Center, has said:

> An alcoholic would be brought to the hospital with, say, beriberi or polyneuropathy, a disease known to be due to nutritional deficiency. An examination of his diet might show that he was obtaining the nutritive elements that would keep a normal man from having this disease—and yet he had it. It was therefore thought that the direct action of alcohol produced the condition. We now know that this is not true. He had a dietary deficiency, but we did not then recognize it, because we did not know about the so-called vitamin-calorie ratio. The average American diet contains about 2500 calories. As judged on a certain scale for measuring vitamin B_1, called "milligrams equivalent," this average American diet provides about 6800 milligrams equivalent of vitamin B_1. The vitamin-calorie ratio—the number of milligrams equivalent of the vitamin divided by the number of calories—thus equals approximately 2.7, as shown in the following equation:
>
> $$\frac{\text{Vitamins } 6,800}{\text{Calories } 2,500} = 2.7$$

If this ratio falls below 1.7 for the average diet of a population group—as it will if the foods eaten contain too little vitamin B_1—there will be a high incidence of beriberi. If the ratio is above 2.5, then there will be a very low incidence of beriberi. Now, for illustration, a certain man eating the average American diet, and therefore obtaining enough nutrients to remain free from beriberi, adds to this diet a pint of whiskey a day. There will then be added to the denominator of the fraction 1600 calories, but there will be added to the numerator no more vitamins. The equation now becomes:

$$\frac{\text{Vitamins } 6{,}800}{\text{Calories } 4{,}100} = 1.66$$

Thus, without cutting down on what has been his normal intake of vitamins, but only by increasing his calories, he has reduced the ratio to the point where he will develop some signs of vitamin B_1 deficiency. The need for certain vitamins, especially the so-called B vitamins, increases with the calories in the diet.

(Quoted in *The Neutral Spirit,* by Berton Roueché)

Not only does alcohol reduce your vitamin-calorie ratio, but it has also a diuretic effect, which further depletes the body of minerals and water-soluble vitamins by flushing them out of the system (as does drinking many cups of coffee or unusually large amounts of water). Drinkers who take as little as two drinks per day, for instance, will excrete from three to five times more magnesium (an important mineral) in their urine than they will when not drinking. A similar flushing effect is exerted on the B vitamins and to a lesser extent on vitamin C.

Furthermore, the vitamin dosages recommended by most conventional medical sources are those supposedly sufficient to prevent symptoms of clinical deficiency, not those sufficient to provide full tissue saturation. Many drinkers who think they are well nourished because they eat an average diet, perhaps supplemented by a one-a-day vitamin pill, are actually walking around with multiple "subclinical" deficiencies. If you suffer from frequent "morning after" symptoms such as fatigue, irritability, nervousness or shakiness, loss of appetite, lack of energy and depression, it's quite likely that those symptoms may be caused by nutritional factors.

Let's imagine someone who has managed to acquire a large proportion of the panoply of ills which alcoholic nutritional deficiency can bring. (Actually, this fellow is not entirely imaginary—you can find him often wandering around Skid Row; more respectable drinkers seldom get quite so far gone.)

Our drunk is suffering from weakness and fatigue, with inexplicable pains in various parts of the body. He walks stiffly and uncertainly and has burning sensations in the soles of his feet. The legs may be swollen with dropsy and the heart muscle impaired. His mind is confused and tends to wander. He also suffers eye trouble, loss of appetite and constipation or diarrhea (general deficiencies but especially of *vitamin B₁*).

He has a red nose, burning or itching eyes, an inflamed tongue, lesions of the mouth *(vitamin B₂,* and probably *C)*. Also anemia *(B₂, folic acid* and possibly *B₁₂)*, and poor resistance to stress and infection *(B₂, A, C)*. His hands and wrists are red and blotchy, with ulcerous sores that become aggravated when exposed to sunlight *(niacin)*. He is irritable *(niacin, C,* perhaps *B₆)*, somewhat mentally deranged *(B₁, niacin, magnesium)*, and suffers from insomnia *(niacin, pantothenic acid, calcium)*. His metabolic functions are disordered *(B₆)*. He bruises easily and has swollen, bleeding gums *(C)*. He has the "shakes," suffers muscle cramps, and sometimes goes into convulsions *(magnesium)*. He has leg ulcers that will not heal and his sexual organs are shrunken and dysfunctional *(zinc)*.

This picture may be rather impressionistic, but the fact is that all the symptoms mentioned are due not to drinking but to the lack of nutrition caused by drinking. And a more moderate, better-fed drinker may still develop many of these symptoms.

Some drinkers become ready victims of malnutrition, while others are seemingly immune though their alcoholic intake may be large. Dr. Roger J. Williams calls this phenomenon *biochemical individuality*. Each individual has a different internal body chemistry, which in turn creates different susceptibilities and resistances. In the days of sailing ships, for instance, ships' crews had to exist for months on vitamin C–deficient diets. Some of the men fell mildly ill of scurvy, some severely ill, and some died . . . but many were quite free of any symptoms!

What this means is that, biochemically speaking, there is no such thing as a "normal" individual. As Dr. Williams says, "Whenever we look for evidences of biochemical individuality we find them, whether in the digestive tract, the blood, the circulatory system, the liver, the system of endocrine glands or in the nervous system. In a table giving the ranges of 36 organic constituents of normal blood, there are 11 items for which the range is 10-fold or more. . . . In some cases the reported ranges are 30, 50 or 80-fold."

Likewise, a person's vitamin requirements may vary 10-fold, 100-fold, or even more. One person may remain perfectly healthy on an intake of 30 milligrams or less of vitamin C, while another may need 300, and still another, 3,000. One cannot, therefore, talk about "normal" nutritional requirements.

Alcohol is a food which contains more "empty" calories than sugar or starch—7 calories per gram as opposed to 4 calories per gram for the carbohydrates. If you drink on the average a half pint of liquor per day, you're getting 800 calories from it. This means that if your daily calorie requirements are 2,000 you're getting 40 percent of them in the form of alcohol; if you need 2,500 calories per day, then alcohol is supplying 32 percent; for 3,000 calories, 26 percent. Double the quantity of alcohol consumed, and the ratio becomes alarmingly high: 80 percent for the person requiring 2,000 calories, 64 percent for the 2,500-calorie person, 52 percent for the 3,000-calorie person.

Obviously, for someone awash in so many booze calories, the food he consumes must be super-nutritious. Since you're getting all the naked calories you can possibly use—and more—from alcohol, the food you eat should consist as much as possible of natural, unprocessed foods, in a diet which is high in protein, moderate in fat and low in carbohydrates. Vitamin-mineral supplementation is important, but as many authorities have pointed out, our knowledge of vitamins is by no means complete. There are perhaps some or even many vitamins still to be discovered—vitamins just as important to health as the ones we know about already and maybe even specifically important to the metabolism of alcohol. So our first line of defense against booze should be eating a good healthy variety of natural foods.

The Drinker's Diet

"YES" FOODS

Eat all you want of (in as much variety as possible):

Fresh fruits of all kinds
Fresh vegetables of all kinds
Meat, fish, poultry, shellfish (liver, which is especially rich in nutrients, should be eaten once a week or more)
Cheese, cottage cheese, skim milk, butter, yogurt, buttermilk
Nuts and nut butter
Oil and salad dressing
Whole grains (undegerminated) and whole-grain breads

"NO" FOODS

To be avoided or eaten sparingly:

Sugar, honey, candy
Sweetened canned fruits
Rice, noodles, macaroni, spaghetti
Dried or canned beans
Packaged, processed or convenience foods of all kinds
Bread, cake and other bakery goods made with refined or bleached flour
Soft drinks, sweetened canned or frozen juices
In addition, stimulants such as coffee or tea should be kept to a minimum

Let's see what this regimen might mean in terms of sample menus.

"Yes" Breakfasts

Fresh fruit or juice
Canned or frozen unsweetened juice
Eggs, any style, with ham or crisp bacon
Meat, poultry or fish
Whole-grain bread or cereal
Black coffee with skim milk and artificial sweetener if desired

"No" Breakfasts

Canned sweetened fruit or juice
Cereal with milk and sugar
Pancakes or waffles with syrup
Toast or muffins with jelly
Eggs with potatoes or grits
Corned-beef hash
Coffee with cream and sugar

"Yes" Lunches

Tomato juice or clear broth
Broiled meat or fish
Chef's salad
Cottage cheese with fresh fruit
Chicken, tuna or lobster salad on whole wheat bread, or no bread at all

"No" Lunches

Thickened soups or soups with noodles
Hot turkey, ham or roast beef sandwich with gravy and potatoes
Hamburger and french fries
Frankfurter and beans, or frankfurter on a bun
Hero sandwich
Desserts
Soft drinks
Coffee or tea with cream and sugar

"Yes" Dinners

Celery and radishes or artichoke hearts
Broth or consommé
Roast beef, steak or chops (clear gravy only)
Fish any style but deep fried
Small potato baked or boiled in skin

"No" Dinners

Fruit cup with canned fruits and syrup
Creamy or starchy soups—vichyssoise, bean soup
TV dinners
Chicken or beef pot pies
Turkey with stuffing and gravy
Hash

Generous helping of one or two vegetables such as cabbage, cauliflower, Brussels sprouts, carrots, zucchini, summer squash, spinach	Creamed meat or fish on toast Thickened gravies Creamed corn Noodles or pasta Desserts of all kinds
Salad	Coffee or tea with sugar and cream
Fresh fruit or cheese for dessert	
Black coffee, no sugar	

The object of the drinker's diet is to get an adequate supply of protein (about 60 grams per day for the average adult) plus a large supply of vegetables which are rich in vitamins and minerals and low in carbohydrates, plus some fruits, plus a minimum of carbohydrate-rich foods. An average serving of meat, poultry or fish contains approximately 20 grams of protein so this amount should be consumed three times daily, or else somewhat larger portions eaten at the main meal. Another way to make sure that you get adequate protein is to supplement meat, eggs or fish with cottage cheese, which is quite high in protein, or to drink several glasses of skim milk every day. Homogenized whole milk is not recommended for adults, for reasons we'll discuss in the section called "Alcohol and Your Heart."

Eating-out tips

It's easy enough to follow the drinker's diet even in "ethnic" restaurants if you order dishes high in protein and low in carbohydrates and try to get some fresh vegetables with your meal. Here are some samples of what to order.

ITALIAN RESTAURANTS

'Yes" Dishes	"No" Dishes
Veal piccata	Minestrone
Steak pizzaiola	All pasta—spaghetti, cannelloni,
Shrimp scampi	ravioli

Roast veal
Kidney sauté
Eggplant parmigiana
Fish stew (zuppa di pesce)
Prosciutto and melon
Salad
Antipasto

Polenta
Risotto
Pizza
Stuffed peppers
Stuffed clams
Desserts

CHINESE RESTAURANTS

"Yes" Dishes	*"No"* Dishes
Pork, chichen, shrimp or beef with Chinese vegetables, broccoli or green pepper	Sweet and sour dishes
	Fried rice
	Noodles and wonton
Steamed fish	Fried shrimp
Bean curd with meat or fish	Dumplings
Mustard-green soup	Shrimp balls
Egg-drop soup	Egg rolls
Seaweed soup	Egg foo yong
Chop suey	Shrimp with lobster sauce
Moo goo gai pan	Chow mein
Minimum of white rice	

FRENCH RESTAURANTS

"Yes" Dishes	*"No"* Dishes
Clear soups	Cream soups
Mixed hors d'oeuvres	Onion soup
Mushrooms à la grecque	Blanquette of veal
Asparagus vinaigrette	Quenelles
Roast chicken	Coquilles St. Jacques
Leg of lamb	Beef Wellington
Broiled steak or chops	Seafood crêpes
Mixed grill	Stews and ragouts
Broiled liver or kidney	Lobster thermidor
Broiled fish	Quiches
Salad	Desserts
Cheeses	
Black coffee	

If you're used to a lot of sugar and starches in your diet, this drinker's diet may seem unsatisfying at first. We're all more or less creatures of habit, and what we're used to *seems* right even though it may be quite wrong for us. Actually, the fact that the drinker's diet feels wrong to you may be a strong indication that your present diet is a bad one. Many drinkers experience a mild to severe hypoglycemic (low blood sugar) effect due to the quantities of alcohol they ingest and to a high carbohydrate diet. If on the drinker's diet you should find yourself craving sugar, this is a strong indication that perhaps you are somewhat hypoglycemic. In this case you should make a distinct effort to get plenty of protein. Adding a scoop or two of cottage cheese to your breakfast and/or lunch and drinking a glass of skim milk several times a day between meals is a good way to increase protein consumption.

Taking extra vitamins and minerals

As I've mentioned, conventional medical thinking views vitamins as something to be taken in order to prevent deficiencies rather than to promote optimum health. This is unfortunate for us humans. Animal doctors do not take a similar view. Any veterinarian or animal breeder knows from daily experience that well-fed animals thrive while ill-fed animals do not. Well-fed cattle or poultry grow rapidly, breed well and have few diseases. Ill-fed animals are sickly, either breeding not at all or giving birth to feeble or defective offspring, and their rate of growth is quite poor. The Food and Nutrition Board of the National Research Council of the National Academy of Sciences takes a very cautious view of the vitamin requirements of humans—45 milligrams of vitamin C is the recommended daily allowance for a 154-pound man. The same board, however, has a Committee on Animal Nutrition, and their recommendations are much higher; for the monkey, the recommendation is 55 milligrams per kilo of body weight. Thus a 154-pound monkey would receive 3,850 milligrams of vitamin C. There seem to be two standards here: partial nutrition for humans; full nutrition for animals. Lucky animals!

Let's see how we can go about getting a full supply of vitamins and minerals. Since Dr. Roger Williams is perhaps the world's greatest authority on nutrition and alcohol, why don't we start with his recommendations for a daily supplement?

VITAMINS

Vitamin A	20,000 units	Niacinamide	40 mg.
Vitamin D	1,000 units	Pantothenate	40 mg.
Ascorbic acid	200 mg.	Vitamin B_{12}	10 mcg.
Thiamine (B_1)	4 mg.	Vitamin E (tocopherol)	10 mg.
Riboflavin (B_2)	4 mg.	Inositol	200 mg.
Pyridoxine (B_6)	6 mg.		
Choline	200 mg.		

MINERALS

Calcium	300 mg.	Iodine	0.1 mg.
Phosphate	250 mg.	Iron	10 mg.
Magnesium	100 mg.	Manganese	1 mg.
Copper	1 mg.	Zinc	5 mg.

Dr. Williams comments: "This supplement is not tailored to any particular individual's needs. It is recommended to anyone who wishes to help give his body (and brain) cells better nutrition. This better nutrition may be of benefit in any number of diseased conditions including alcoholism."

Although formulated fairly recently, this supplement cannot now be purchased in its entirety without prescription. The Food and Drug Administration, which in its regulation of vitamins seems to follow the banana-peel philosophy (some persons slip on banana peels, therefore the sale of bananas must be outlawed), has restricted the sale of vitamins A and D to quantities not exceeding 10,000 units of A and 400 units of D. By taking two A-and-D capsules, however, one can get 20,000 units of A and 800 of D, close enough to the original formulation.

Missing entirely from the Williams formula is one important

B vitamin—folic acid. The FDA does not allow it to be sold in any significant amount. Folic acid, of which Dr. Di Cyan says deficiencies are "frequent," especially among alcoholics and pregnant women, masks the effects of pernicious anemia (a B_{12} deficiency disease) by curing the anemia but allowing the neurologically degenerative effects of the disease to proceed. Pernicious anemia is usually found only among extreme vegetarians who will not touch meat, eggs or dairy products or in people who have a genetic factor that prevents them from absorbing or utilizing B_{12}. Folic acid assists in the growth of red blood cells, is necessary for the division of all body cells, and is essential for the production of RNA and DNA. It is needed in the production of antibodies to prevent infections and for the utilization of sugar and amino acids. Yet, according to one survey, folic-acid deficiency is more common in hospital patients than deficiencies of any other vitamin. One milligram of folic acid would be sensible in a normal supplement—5 milligrams for persons suffering from alcoholic anemia—yet at the present time the most the FDA will allow to be sold is 0.4 mg.* So every drinker should make a point of eating *something* rich in folic acid every day: liver, kidney, nuts, wheat germ, leafy green vegetables.

For drinkers who may be suffering drastic deficiencies or whose vitamin requirements are unusually high, larger doses of vitamins can be helpful. Here are some sample dosages used in megavitamin therapy.

Vitamin A	20,000 units	Vitamin B_3 (niacin)	200–1,000 mg.
Vitamin D	800 units	Vitamin B_6	100–400 mg.
Vitamin E	200–600 units	Choline	250–1,000 mg.
Vitamin C	1,000–5,000 mg.	Inositol	500–1,000 mg.
Vitamin B_1	100–300 mg.	Pantothenate	100–200 mg.
Vitamin B_2	50–100 mg.		

*Folic acid is sold only in combination with B_{12}. It is possible to buy tablets containing 0.4 mg. folic acid and 25 mcg. B_{12}. Three of these daily will provide 1.2 mg. folic acid.

You'll have to decide for yourself how much vitamin supplementation you need. A drinker whose ratio of alcohol calories to food calories is not extreme will probably get sufficient protection against deficiencies from the Williams formula. Someone who drinks heavily may need dosages closer to the megavitamin range. A drinker who is severely rundown should consult a doctor—persons with marked B-vitamin deficiencies are often unable to absorb these vitamins properly when taken by mouth and will need intravenous injections of them.

CHECK LIST OF VITAMINS AND MINERALS

Fat-soluble vitamins

(Note: Fat-soluble vitamins cannot be stored in the body unless eaten together with fat-containing foods. Multivitamin capsules, therefore, should be taken with or directly after meals.)

Vitamin A, found in: liver, kidney, heart, seafood, milk, egg yolk, fortified margarine, broccoli, Brussels sprouts, cabbage, carrots, escarole, kale, lettuce, spinach, tomatoes, other yellow and green vegetables.

Symptoms of deficiency: poor vision, night blindness, dryness of skin and hair, acne, poor resistance to infection, poor healing of wounds, hormone deficiencies.

Deficiencies in drinkers: frequent.

Optimum daily dosage: 20,000 units.

Toxicity: in infants, possible if overlarge doses are given. Adults can only incur poisoning if improbably large amounts are consumed. Many ordinary foods contain large amounts of vitamin A—¼ pound of beef liver, for instance, has 43,000 units.

Vitamin D, found in: fish-liver oils, D-fortified milk. Vitamin D is also produced in the body by exposure to sunlight.

Symptoms of deficiency: softening of the bones, inability to absorb calcium.

Deficiencies in drinkers: infrequent.

Optimum daily dosage: 400–1,000 units.

Toxicity: D is toxic in large doses. Do not take more than 1,000 units except under a doctor's direction.

Vitamin E, found in: wheat germ, beef liver, nuts, fruit, leafy green vegetables, vegetable oils.

Symptoms of deficiency: premature aging, infertility, anemia, liver and kidney damage, enlarged prostate, muscle damage.

Deficiencies in drinkers: some, but usually mild rather than severe.

Optimum daily dosage: 30 mg.

Toxicity: none. (Note: Vitamin E and iron are mutually incompatible. If you're taking a vitamin-mineral capsule containing iron, supplemental E should be taken eight hours before or after the iron.)

Vitamin K found in: liver, leafy green vegetables, cow's milk, vegetable oils.

Symptoms of deficiency: poor blood clotting, easy bruising, hemorrhage, poor healing of wounds.

Deficiencies in drinkers: rare.

Dosage: synthesized by bacteria in the intestine. Supplementation is usually needed only in extraordinary circumstances and should be given only by a doctor.

Water-soluble vitamins

Vitamin B complex. The vitamins in this group are perhaps the most important to a drinker. As we have seen, they are easily washed out of the tissues by the diuretic effects of alcohol; also, the extra calories in alcohol produce a demand for extra B vitamins. The B vitamins are necessary to every cell in the body, and are distributed throughout the body equally. Thus, considerable deficiencies can exist without showing up as abnormalities in any specific organ; only when the deficiency becomes severe will it manifest itself in a particular group of cells.

Vitamin B₁ (thiamine) found in: whole-grain breads and cereals, yeast, liver, lean pork, fresh green vegetables.

Symptoms of deficiency: weakness and fatigue, muscle cramps, inexplicable pains in various parts of the body, burning sensations in the soles of the feet, constipation or diarrhea, difficulty in walking, loss of appetite, weight loss, mental confusion, heart trouble, paralysis, aggravation of an existing diabetic condition, aggravation of vitamin A deficiency.

Deficiencies in drinkers: very frequent.

Dosage: RDA,* 1.5 mg. Reasonable higher dosage: 5–50 mg.

Toxicity: virtually none, except when large doses are repeatedly taken in the absence of the other B vitamins. In such case, the deficiencies of the other B vitamins will be amplified and aggravated.

Vitamin B₂ (riboflavin) found in: whole-grain products, liver, lean meat, fresh green vegetables, eggs, milk and other dairy products.

Symptoms of deficiency: inflammation of the tongue, lesions of the mouth, anemia, malfunction of the eyes, poor resistance to stress and infection.

Deficiencies in drinkers: frequent.

Dosage: RDA, 1.7 mg. Reasonable higher dosage: 5–50 mg.

Toxicity: same as B₁.

Vitamin B₃ (niacin) found in: liver and lean meat, eggs, milk and other dairy foods, whole-grain products, yeast, fish, peanuts.

Symptoms of deficiency: inflammation of tongue and mouth, skin changes, diarrhea, weakness, headache, irritability, insomnia, mental confusion.

Deficiencies in drinkers: frequent.

Dosage: RDA, 20 mg. Reasonable higher dosage: 50–400 mg.

Toxicity: same as B₁.

*Recommended Daily Allowance, as published by the Food and Drug Administration.

Vitamin B₆ (pyridoxine) found in: wheat germ, liver, kidney, lean meat, fish, bananas, avocados, raisins and prunes, yeast, nuts, soybeans.

Symptoms of deficiency: Fatigue, eczema-like skin outbreaks, conjunctivitis, irritability, poor memory, convulsions.

Deficiencies in drinkers: frequent.

Dosage: RDA, 2 mg. Reasonable higher dosage: 5–100 mg.

Toxicity: none.

Pantothenic acid found in: liver, kidney, heart, wheat germ, yeast, green vegetables.

Symptoms of deficiency: aggravation of allergic reactions, nervousness, digestive disturbances, depression, irritability, increased need for sleep, numb sensations in arms and legs, incoordination, muscle spasm.

Deficiencies in drinkers: very frequent.

Dosage: RDA, 10 mg. Reasonable higher dosage: 50–100 mg.

Toxicity: same as B_1.

Biotin found in: liver, kidney, yeast, egg yolks, fresh vegetables.

Symptoms of deficiency: muscle pain, lethargy, skin outbreaks, gastrointestinal disturbances.

Deficiencies in drinkers: infrequent.

Dosage: RDA, .3 mg. Higher dosage: .4–1 mg.

Toxicity: same as B_1. (Note: Along with some other vitamins, biotin is synthesized in the intestine by the action of bacteria. When the bacterial population of the intestine has been depleted by antibiotics, it can be restored by eating yogurt or other soured-milk products, such as cultured buttermilk.)

Folic acid found in: wheat germ and bran, liver, kidney, leafy green vegetables, nuts.

Symptoms of deficiency: anemia, paleness, dizziness, depression, shortness of breath.

Deficiencies in drinkers: very frequent.

Dosage: RDA, .4 mg. Reasonable higher dosage: 1–2 mg.

Toxicity: none, except in cases of pernicious anemia when folic acid is given without B_{12}.

Vitamin B_{12} found in: liver, kidney and other organ meats, oysters and shellfish, cheese, milk and eggs.

Symptoms of deficiency: pernicious anemia, leading to fatigue, poor appetite, neurological disturbances, intestinal disturbances.

Deficiencies in drinkers: yes, but usually mild.

Dosage: RDA, 6 mcg. Reasonable higher dosage: 10–50 mcg. (Note: a full-fledged B_{12} deficiency is a serious condition which needs to be treated by injection rather than oral doses of the vitamin. A physician should be consulted.)

Toxicity: none.

Included in the B-complex group are the following substances which are not officially classified as vitamins:

PABA (para-aminobenzoic acid) found in: liver, yeast, wheat germ.

Symptoms of deficiency: eczema, premature graying of hair, poor tolerance of sunlight.

Deficiencies in drinkers: occasional.

Dosage: no RDA. Reasonable dosage: 100–400 mg.

Toxicity: none, except that it interferes with the therapeutic effect of sulfa drugs. Since sulfa is rarely prescribed, this is no longer a problem.

Choline found in: brains, liver, yeast, wheat germ, lecithin, egg yolk.

Symptoms of deficiency: fatty liver, kidney damage, high blood pressure, stomach ulcers.

Deficiencies in drinkers: occasional.

Dosage: no RDA. Reasonable dosage: 200–1,000 mg.

Toxicity: none.

Inositol found in: liver, yeast, lecithin, wheat germ, oatmeal, corn, dark molasses.

Symptoms of deficiency: eczema, constipation, hair loss, nerve disorders.

Deficiencies in drinkers: occasional.

Dosage: no RDA. Reasonable dosage: 200–1,000 mg.

Toxicity: none.

Vitamin C found in: vegetables, citrus fruits, liver.

Symptoms of deficiency: fatigue and irritability, lack of resistance to stress and infection, easy bruising due to weakness of small blood vessels, weakness, swollen and bleeding gums.

Deficiencies in drinkers: frequent.

Dosage: RDA, 60 mg. Reasonable higher dosage: 200–4,000 mg.

Toxicity: none.

Minerals

Calcium found in: milk and milk products (the best food source). This mineral and phosphorus are interdependent; each works only in combination with the other. Phosphorus should not be taken as a supplement, however, since most foods contain an excess of phosphorus over calcium.

Symptoms of deficiency: insomnia, irritability, poor blood clotting, depression, tooth decay, bone weakness.

Deficiencies in drinkers: frequent, especially in combination with magnesium deficiency.

Dosage: 300–1,000 mg. (The RDA is 1,000 mg.)

Toxicity: none, but excessive calcium taken with excessive vitamin D may cause calcification of the bones.

Magnesium found in: meat, seafood, nuts, wheat germ and bran, kelp.

Symptoms of deficiency: nervousness, muscle spasm and

twitching, mental confusion, convulsions, delirium tremens, brain damage.

Deficiencies in drinkers: frequent.

Dosage: RDA, 400 mg. Reasonable higher dosage: 500–800 mg.

Toxicity: usually confined to people taking excessive amounts of Epsom salt (magnesium sulfate).

Iron found in: meat, eggs, fruit, vegetables, wheat germ and bran.

Symptoms of deficiency: iron-deficiency anemia.

Deficiencies in drinkers: occasional.

Dosage: RDA, 18 mg. Higher dosage: 30–100 mg.

Toxicity: iron is poisonous in large amounts, so iron supplements should never be taken indiscriminately.

Copper found in: shellfish, liver, peas and nuts.

Symptoms of deficiency: anemia, impaired absorption of iron.

Deficiencies in drinkers: rare.

Dosage: RDA, 2 mg.

Toxicity: some.

Iodine found in: seafood and sea fish, kelp, spinach.

Symptoms of deficiency: impaired thyroid function, goiter.

Deficiencies in drinkers: occasional mild deficiencies.

Dosage: RDA, 150 mcg. Reasonable higher dosage: 1–2 mg.

Toxicity: poisonous in large amounts.

Zinc found in: seafood, liver, wheat germ and bran, peas and nuts.

Symptoms of deficiency: bone deformities, leg ulcers, loss of taste and/or smell, dysfunction of male reproductive organs, possible relationship with heart attack, pneumonia, kidney disease.

Deficiencies in drinkers: frequent.

Dosage: RDA, 15 mg.

Toxicity: only in large amounts.

A final word

When taking vitamins, especially the larger doses, it is well to preserve a skeptical, experimental frame of mind. Some people are believers—they've read that vitamins are a magic means to perfect health and keep stuffing themselves with ever-increasing numbers of tablets and capsules, hoping to achieve some sort of nutritional nirvana or to correct a condition which has nothing to do with nutrition, such as a disease or organic defect or a flabby, sedentary physique. Others are disbelievers who feel vitamins and health foods are only for nuts and kooks and that one can survive perfectly well on a diet of hamburgers, pop tarts and TV dinners. A vitamin deficiency is an actual, *real* condition—either you have it or you don't. If you do, taking the appropriate vitamins will improve your health. And, if you don't, vitamins will do nothing for you, even if you buy out the whole store.

If you can find a doctor who is genuinely interested in full nutrition, and can afford his fees, you can avoid a lot of hit-or-miss experimentation. The medically trained practitioner has ways of accurately determining whether or not deficiencies exist—either by blood analyses, or by giving doses of various vitamins, then checking to see if the dose is largely excreted (in which case there's no shortage of the substance in the tissues) or largely retained (indicating there is a shortage).

Glutamine and niacinamide: possible cures for alcoholism

Roger Williams and a colleague of his, William Shive, have suggested that an amino acid named glutamine, which is present in proteins but often converted to glutamic acid during digestion, might be useful in treating the craving for drink. Glutamine protects bacteria against alcohol poisoning, and when given to rats decreases their voluntary alcohol consumption. Anyone who is having trouble controlling his drinking might do well to try glutamine, which is a harmless, tasteless food substance. Human trials have been limited so far, but in some cases alcoholics have voluntarily stopped drinking when given glutamine without knowing they were getting it. The suggested adult dose is 2 grams per day. Glutamine is the only amino acid which readily passes the blood-brain barrier, and the theory is that better nutrition of the brain reduces the craving for alcohol.

Niacinamide therapy has proved helpful to many alcoholics. This is the same therapy that has produced significant results in treating schizophrenia and other "mental diseases." Two thousand mg. of niacinamide, together with the same amount of vitamin C, are given twice or three times a day together with an adequate multivitamin-mineral supplement. In some subjects no improvement takes place. In others, dramatic results occur. The reason for taking niacinamide rather than niacin is that niacin produces an uncomfortable flushing of the skin when taken in large doses.

6

The Overweight Problem: Coping with Those Extra Calories

A DRINKER WOULD seem to have two choices: eat a normal diet and get fat, or cut his food intake and be malnourished. Of the two, the first choice seems preferable, particularly if one's drinking tends to be heavy rather than light. A thin person lives on a tight metabolic budget and easily depletes his reserves of energy and nutriments. Heavy drinking is much more apt to disturb him than it will a fleshier person. Of the thirty-five or so heavy drinkers I interviewed, only six were decidedly thin, and four of these seemed to have more than their share of alcoholic problems: inability to "handle" liquor, with frequent descents into Stage Three and Stage Four while the rest of the crowd was enjoying itself; hangover symptoms that sounded like incipient polyneuritis; blackouts and minor accidents that happened more often than with heftier drinkers. Heavy drinking, after all, is a sort of gastrointestinal athleticism. The typical alcoholic athlete tends to be tubby, like a Sumo wrestler, or at least on the fleshy side of "normal" for his height and frame.

Is it possible, though, to drink, remain healthy, and yet be slim? Yes, but the difficulty of doing so is directly proportionate to the amount you drink. On two drinks a day, you're adding about 270 calories to your intake . . . four drinks, 540 calories . . . a pint of booze, over 1,400 calories. Obviously, only extraordinary measures can keep down the weight of a pint-a-day person.

Figuring your calorie surplus

Do you have an extra-calorie problem, and if so, how large is it? To find out, we need to determine how many of the calories you consume are actually surplus. This is done by comparing your daily calorie requirement with the number of calories you actually consume.

Finding the calorie requirement. A reasonably accurate method of determining how many calories you need is to multiply your body weight by 15. (A 160-pound man needs about 160 × 15 or 2,400 calories daily.) The 15-calories-per-pound-of-body-weight figure applies to everyone whose energy expenditures are in the sedentary to moderately-active range. If you spend most of your day in actual physical labor or the equivalent (hod carrying, stone masoning, carpentry) you may need 20 to 25 calories per pound, depending on how strenuous and prolonged your exertions are.

Average food intake. Count up the food calories you consume. Below is a somewhat abbreviated calorie chart. (More complete ones are available in booklet form on every newsstand.) Add up the calorie values for everything you ate in the last twenty-four hours. Don't forget the butter on your bread, the sugar in your coffee, all stray snacks and tidbits. (If you don't trust your memory to reconstruct food intake, keep a diary for a day or two, listing everything you eat.)

CALORIE COUNTER

Average Serving	*Calorie Count*
Bread and Cereals	
White Bread (1 slice)	65
Whole-wheat bread (1 slice)	55

Doughnut (1)	135
Macaroni with cheese (1 cup)	475
Rice (1 cup)	200

Beverages
Coffee or tea (plain)	0
Carbonated beverage (8 oz.)	105

Dairy Foods
Milk, whole (1 cup)	165
Milk, skim (1 cup)	90
Malted milk (2 cups)	560
Butter (1 T*)	100
Cheese, cheddar (1 oz.)	115
Cheese, cottage (1 cup)	240
Cream, light (1 T)	30
Cream, whipped, unsweetened (1 T)	25
Egg (1 medium-size)	80

Desserts
Pie, apple (4-in. sector)	330
Pie, custard (4-in. sector)	265
Pie, mince (4-in. sector)	340
Pie, lemon meringue (4-in. sector)	300
Cake, angel food (2-in. sector)	110
Cake, layer (2-in. sector)	320
Brownie (3" × 2" × 2")	295
Ice cream, plain (½ cup)	150
Sherbet (½ cup)	118
Vanilla pudding (1 cup)	285

Fruits
Apple, raw (medium)	70
Banana, raw (medium)	85
Cantaloupe (½)	40
Grapefruit (½ small)	50
Orange, raw (medium)	70
Peach, raw (medium)	35
Pear, raw (medium)	100
Pineapple, canned (1 slice)	95

Fruit Juices
Grapefruit, fresh (1 cup)	85
Orange, fresh (1 cup)	105
Pineapple, canned (1 cup)	120
Tomato, canned (1 cup)	50

*T equals tablespoonful

Average Serving	*Calorie Count*

Vegetables

Beets (1 cup)	70
Broccoli (1 cup)	45
Carrots (1 cup)	45
Corn (1 cup)	65
Peas (1 cup)	110
Potatoes, mashed (1 cup)	145
Spinach (1 cup)	45
Sweet potato, baked	155
Tomato, raw	30

Meat, Fish and Poultry

Beef, sirloin steak (9 oz.)	750
Lamb chop (3 oz.)	450
Pork chop (3 oz.)	295
Ham (3 oz.)	340
Bacon (2 strips)	95
Veal chop (3 oz.)	170
Chicken, canned (3 oz.)	170
Tuna (3 oz.)	170
Sardines (3 oz.)	180
Salmon, canned (3 oz.)	120
Luncheon meat (3 oz.)	165
Frankfurters (2)	300

Miscellaneous

Mayonnaise (1 T)	110
French dressing (1 T)	60
Assorted jams (1 T)	55
Sugar (1 T)	50
Hamburger on a bun	492
Hot dog on a bun	300
Peanut-butter sandwich	220
Cheese sandwich	333
Chocolate nut sundae	350
Cashews (1 oz.)	164
Peanuts, chopped (1 T)	50
Fudge (1 oz.)	116
Chocolate creams (1 oz.)	110

Liquor calories. Now count up how much you drink on the average. Find the caloric value from the list below.

	Calories
1 oz. 100-proof spirits	135
1½ oz. 100-proof spirits	200
1½ oz. 86-proof spirits	135
1½ oz. 80-proof spirits	125
4½ oz. table wine	115
4½ oz. sweet wine	200
Beer, 12 oz.	150
Martini (2 oz., 90-proof)	200
1 pint 80-proof spirits	1,275
1 pint 86-proof spirits	1,445
1 pint 90-proof spirits	1,480
1 pint 100-proof spirits	1,680

Your surplus, if any. Adding up your food and liquor and subtracting from it your daily calorie requirement gives the amount of the surplus. For instance, let's take a 160-pound man (calorie requirement 2,400) who consumes an average of 2,160 food calories plus six drinks (810 calories) daily.

actual calories	2,160
	810
	2,970
minus calorie requirement	2,400
surplus	570

Since it takes approximately 3,500 calories to add a pound of fat to the body, this man will tend to gain a little over a pound a week on his present diet.

Coping with surplus calories

There are four basic ways of eliminating or neutralizing a calorie surplus:

1. Cut down on food
2. Cut down on liquor
3. Burn up the surplus through exercise
4. Reorganize eating and drinking patterns

The Overweight Problem | 73

Let's start with the last of these.

Minimizing the alcohol calories. We've already seen that alcohol contains empty calories which produce energy but cannot of themselves deposit fat in the body.* When we eat and drink we use the alcohol for energy and the food is deposited as fat. Liquor does not always contribute its calories efficiently, however. The very *worst* way to drink, for someone with an overweight problem, is to have cocktails with hors d'oeuvres or snacks, followed by a heavy meal. This virtually insures that you'll burn alcohol for energy most of the evening, while the food you ate turns to fat.

Turn the process around and you have a chance to minimize the weight-augmenting effects of alcohol. This runs counter to all the advice about eating a lot before you drink so you won't get too drunk, but someone who drinks enough to have an alcohol-caused weight problem probably has no need for the precautions of neophyte drinkers.

The idea is to do your heaviest eating early in the day, in the nondrinking hours, so that most food will be digested by the time you begin to drink. Proteins at breakfast, carbohydrates at lunch, and only salad, green vegetables and other roughage for dinner, is the plan. For instance:

Breakfast:	*or:*
fruit juice	½ grapefruit
steak and eggs	liver and bacon
½ cup cottage cheese	hashed brown potatoes
1 slice whole-wheat toast	1 slice toast
coffee or tea	coffee or tea

*Although in rundown, vitamin-deficient drinkers whose blood does not contain sufficient oxygen, some conversion of alcohol to fat may take place. Alcohol turns to acetate in the metabolic process and the acetate molecules are burned up by linking themselves with oxygen molecules. If there is insufficient oxygen to do the job, some of the acetate will be laid down as fat. Adequate intake of vitamins, particularly B_1, B_6, biotin and E, which promote the oxygen level, will help prevent this phenomenon.

Lunch:	*or:*
soup	½ cantaloupe
fruit salad	stuffed avocado
toasted cheese sandwich	apple pie
coffee or tea	coffee or tea

Dinner:	*or:*
tomato juice	mushrooms à la greque
artichoke hearts vinaigrette	cauliflower au gratin
spinach salad	sliced tomatoes

Drinking may begin one half hour before dinner and continue as long as you wish afterward. No snacks of any kind after dinner or before bedtime. If you're used to wolfing down peanut-butter sandwiches, potato chips and other delicacies, do so in the morning between breakfast and lunch, at the coffee-break hour. This regime will insure the most *in*efficient possible use of liquor calories, particularly if you drink rather heavily. Actually, heavy drinking is in itself inefficient, calorie-wise, because, owing to the length of time alcohol stays in the body of the drinker, a lot more of it is excreted—through respiration, urine, etc.—than is the case in more moderate drinking.

Exercise. Are you sedentary? Do you, in other words, spend your working days sitting at a desk, use an automobile to run errands with, have a houseful of motorized gadgets to do your chores for you? Then exercise is the *most* important form of weight control you could possibly undertake.

The sedentary life is physiologically abnormal for both humans and animals. In his book *Overweight,* Dr. Jean Mayer, one of the world's foremost authorities on obesity and weight control, says:

> That an increase in appetite follows an increase in activity in a normal animal or person is true enough. It explains why the weight of most adults is relatively constant. A fine adjustment of appetite prevents the body from burning away its substance when the individual is called upon to perform at a higher level of exertion than

has been his custom. This adjustment of caloric intake to caloric expenditure admits of definite limitations even in a normal person. Energy expenditure must not be raised above a certain upper limit; it must not be lowered below a certain minimal limit.

In the sedentary person, the correlation between physical exertion and appetite has been lost. Sedentary individuals eat more, not less, than those who are "normally" active, and since they have no way to burn off the extra calories, they get fat. For an active person, there is a "cost" to becoming overweight—if he gains a few pounds, he will have to burn up extra calories to carry the increased weight through his usual activities. The sedentary individual, however, will expend much less energy in moving his extra weight around; his weight gain will therefore be much more rapid.

As Dr. Mayer says,

> We . . . sleep all night in comfortable beds, ride to work, sit all day in front of our desks, or stand before our work benches. We ride back home, sit before the dinner table, sit to read our papers and magazines, sit at a motion picture or in front of our television set—and so to bed. We are using our bodies and their marvelous regulatory mechanisms in a way for which they were never designed. Small wonder that, living thus on the fat of the land, many of us become fat. The wonder is that, for many others, appetite does adjust to this extraordinary set of circumstances.

A sedentary person is an unhealthy person. It's not just that he's apt to be flabby and overweight. He's weak, physically clumsy and inept, less resistant to disease and infection. Less resistant, also, to the effects of toxins such as alcohol and tobacco. A sedentary individual who smokes and drinks heavily runs the risk of taking many more years off his life than an active individual with the same vices. Even disregarding the increased mortality rate, sedentariness is sad because it culminates in a sort of living death. We're all familiar with people in their fifties and sixties who have ceased being viable physical organisms—to them, getting up out of a chair, climbing a flight of stairs, getting in or out of a car are arduous if not semi-impossible activities.

The sedentary person is particularly prone to heart disease. As Dr. Laurence E. Morehouse says in his book *Total Fitness*,

> When a sedentary person becomes fairly active by adding a mild exercise such as walking, many changes take place in his body that can be inferred to be important in developing his resistance to cardiac disease. Blood pressure is lowered, resting heart rate decreases, muscles—including the heart muscle—become stronger, there is a vast increase in the number of active small blood vessels which carry blood to the cells of the muscular tissues. The blood itself is improved; it carries more oxygen, and the blood platelets, which become sticky and plug up vessels in the heart and brain, thereby causing heart attacks and strokes, become less sticky with exercise training.

Becoming unsedentary. Any activity involving more than his usual exertion will improve the condition of a sedentary person: walking up and down stairs rather than using the elevator, walking or bicycling to the corner store rather than driving there in a car, mowing the lawn or puttering around the garden, carrying something heavy, sawing wood, dancing, swimming, playing ping pong, shoveling snow . . . the list is endless.

Walking is the most basic activity for anyone with two legs and is probably the best for people who are middle-aged and/or severely out of shape. Dr. Harry Johnson of the Life Extension Institute recommends walking as the only form of exercise for his middle-aged patients. He advises three brisk twenty-minute walks every day (or two thirty-minute walks or one one-hour walk). When his patients ask him where they can find the time for this, he asks them, "Where do you find the time to eat three meals a day?" If your muscles are badly deteriorated, of course, it may take you weeks or months to get yourself in shape to take a brisk two-to-three-mile walk, but it's well worth making the effort. As Dr. Morehouse says,

Muscles are the engines that move you. The fuels for the engines are chemicals the body constantly renews. These fuels are useless unless they have engines that are capable of functioning. If you don't use a muscle, it wastes away until it all but disappears. Each fiber shrinks to almost nothing. Yet the moment you start to use it again, it's like breathing on a bed of coals. It lights up, ignites. If you're one who has let himself go for twenty years, just try walking around the block. It's like a miracle. Where you thought there was nothing, strength reappears.

I remember years ago reading a newspaper interview with the financial "whiz kid" Beardsley Ruml, who at barely thirty was made chairman of R. H. Macy & Co. and later became head of the Federal Reserve Bank. Mr. Ruml explained why he never took any exercise: "I plan to lead an entirely cerebral, sedentary life, and I believe I'll live longer if I don't let my body get accustomed to any form of exertion." Mr. Ruml may have been terribly smart with money, but he was a poor guesser about his own health—he died of heart failure at the age of sixty-one.

Once you're in shape, staying there can be done easily. Dr. Morehouse lists five activities necessary for minimum maintenance (preventing any physical deterioration):

1. Turn and twist your body joints to their near-maximum range of motion.

2. Stand for a total of two hours per day.

3. Lift something unusually heavy for five seconds.

4. Get your heart rate up to 120 beats a minute for at least three minutes.

5. Burn up 300 calories a day in physical activity.

"COST" OF VARIOUS ACTIVITIES IN CALORIES

Activity	Calories per hour
Walking slowly	120
Walking moderately fast	250–300
Walking very fast	400–500
Bicycling (depending on speed)	250–450
Running (depending on speed)	800–1,500
Swimming (depending on speed)	300–1,500
Golf (no cart)	300

Tennis	400–500
Rowing	1,000–1,500
Ping pong	350–500
Dancing	300–450
Carpentry	150–300
Sawing wood	300–400
Housepainting	150–180
Ironing	50–60
Dishwashing	50–60
Sweeping	80–100
Gardening	150–300

Losing weight via exercise

If you're athletically inclined or a demon for physical exertion, it's entirely possible, of course, to lose as much weight as you choose through exercise alone. This is the way boxers and football players reduce. If you do one hour per day of running, swimming or rowing (briskly, at 1,000 calories per hour), you'll lose two pounds a week. If you're severely overweight—weighing 195, say, when you should weigh 150—then you'll lose *more,* because of the cost of moving those extra 45 pounds around. (You'll lose 2.6 pounds a week.) Strenuous exercise, of course, should only be done by people who are young enough and healthy enough to stand it.

Reducing diets for drinkers

The most famous is the "Drinking Man's Diet," essentially the same plan as those propounded by Dr. Herman *(Calories Don't Count)* Taller, Dr. Irwin *(The Doctor's Quick Weight Loss Diet)* Stillman, and Dr. Robert *(Dr. Atkins Diet Revolution)* Atkins—restricting the diet to protein, fat and roughage, plus 30 grams or less of carbohydrates per day. Eat all the meat, fish, cheese, cottage cheese and butter you want and all the low-carbohydrate vegetables—leafy green vegetables, tomatoes, cauliflower, mushrooms, etc.—nothing starchy or sweet. Drink all the distilled spirits you want and all the dry table wine, but no beer, which contains carbohydrates, or any wine or liquor with sugar in it. I've tried this diet and have talked to at least thirty other drinkers who have also, and found no one who lost as much as he wanted to, although some of the heavier people lost as much as twenty-five pounds. My experience is that I lost about ten pounds (I wanted to lose thirty) and was unable to take off any more even though I persisted on the diet. By this time I was feeling quite uncomfortable and had acute cravings for fruit and potatoes, so I quit.

There are two problems with the low-carbohydrate, high-fat, high-protein diets. One is that because they are so unbalanced they tend to be unhealthy for some people—the high cholesterol content may be bad for people with a tendency to heart problems, for instance, and the large amounts of proteins involved may become toxic to someone with weak kidneys. The other difficulty is that the diet does not re-educate the appetite but encourages the dieter to gorge on less fattening substances.

"Crash" diets. There are many diets designed to take off a lot of weight in a short time, and they work. Having lost the weight, however, most crash dieters put it right back on again. The late Louis Armstrong, for instance, had a pet diet on which he repeatedly lost as much as seventy pounds in a matter of weeks. It involved eating only one large meal ("everything from soup to nuts") at night, then taking a large dose of a laxative called Swiss-Kriss before bed, to flush away the remains of the meal. During the day, Louis ate nothing but sliced tomatoes and took several doses of an antacid, Bisma-Rex, to quiet his stomach. When he got skinny, Louis would go back to eating again and begin ballooning out. In a year or two he would repeat his bizarre diet. In the long run this would seem to have proved unhealthy. Although a vigorous man, Louis died of a heart attack in his sixties.

Author's special. Let me present *my* bizarre crash diet. I'm not recommending it much more than Louis's, but I did lose 40 pounds on it, going from 200 to 160 pounds in about eight weeks.

First: Fast for a day or two, three if you can stand it. This shrinks the stomach and helps you to be satisfied with less food. *Second:* Eat anything you like, but in tiny amounts. Imagine that you're a prisoner in a Nazi concentration camp or stranded on a desert island. Eat only enough to barely survive, supplemented by booze or wine and *lots* of water plus extra vitamins —one "therapeutic dose" multi-vitamin-mineral twice a day with food. Your "menus" might be as follows:

Breakfast
Eat or drink only *one* of the following items:
    glass of orange juice
    cup of coffee with cream and sugar
    slice of buttered toast
    1 egg any style
    1 apple
    5 or 6 cherries
    ½ cup cottage cheese

Lunch
One item only:
    breadless ham sandwich (1 slice ham between 2 slices cheese)
    small bag of peanuts
    glass of wine, no food
    Scotch and soda, no food
    lettuce and tomato salad
    bacon, lettuce and tomato sandwich
    ½ cantaloupe
    slice of watermelon
    slice of cold roast beef
    small shrimp cocktail

Dinner
One item only:
    bowl of soup
    1 baked potato
    small slice of banana cream pie
    1 lamb chop with sliced tomatoes
    small piece of broiled fish

Plus one, several, or many drinks. It's not important *what* you eat; the main thing is to keep your food intake as minuscule as possible during the first two or three weeks when weight loss is greatest, then gradually increase it as losses taper off. I lost ten pounds during my first week, for instance, about six each in the second and third, four in the fourth, three in the fifth, and an average of two each in the sixth, seventh and eighth.

It's a good idea to weigh yourself every day—in the morning just before breakfast is the best time. Seeing the pounds coming off is the best possible reinforcement for continuing on the diet. The great advantage of crash diets is that many people find it easier to make big or "heroic" efforts than to reduce through months or years of little niggling self-denials. Let me say again that I'm not recommending my crash diet. Unless you're in perfect health, you shouldn't try it without asking your doctor first. (He'll probably say "No.")

Calorie-counting diets

There are a number of ways of reducing via calorie counting.

Eating to your ideal weight. Let's say you weigh 168 but would like to weigh 140. You simply consume 140 × 15 or 2,100 calories daily. In time you'll arrive at your desired weight.

1,000 calories off. This is a method used by many weight-control doctors. First you find your daily calorie requirement. Let's say it's 168 × 15 or 2,520. You subtract 1,000 calories from this, leaving 1,520, which is your daily allotment. This diet should produce a weekly loss of about two pounds, but you'll have to keep adjusting as you lose. (After you've lost ten pounds, for instance, your daily intake should be 158 × 15 or 2,370, minus 1,000 equals 1,370.) When you get within ten pounds of your goal—or twenty pounds if you were grossly overweight to begin with—it is probably a good idea to let up the pressure a little and try for only a one-pound weekly loss (500 calories off per day, or 150 × 15 equals 2,250, minus 500 equals 1,750).

One advantage of this method is that you can calculate with a fair degree of accuracy how long it will take to reach your goal if you stick to the diet. For the 168-pounder wanting to reach 140, for instance, the process would take about 19 weeks—nine weeks for the first 18 pounds, ten for the next 10.

Slow-but-sure methods. Many weight-control authorities are of the opinion that only a slow and gradual program of weight reduction is apt to result in permanent loss. Drastic diets are unsettling to the metabolism and do not allow the dieter to become thoroughly habituated to a lesser caloric intake. When the diet ceases, he will tend to revert to his previous eating habits. Dr. Harry Johnson, of the Life Extension Institute, advises not changing one's eating habits or worrying about how many calories one consumes, but simply cutting out about 300 calories daily. In other words, count only the calories you eliminate. It doesn't much matter whether what you eliminate is fat, carbohydrate, alcohol, or even protein. This regime will produce a gradual loss—of about two to three pounds per month.

Cutting down on booze vs. cutting down on food

Which is better? Probably best for your health would be to eliminate mostly alcohol calories. But if you're at all concerned with *permanent* weight loss, you have to consider that if you start drinking again you'll regain what you lost. Cutting out food is not good either—you can't starve yourself indefinitely. Restricting both alcohol and food would seem to be the answer. *How much* of each depends on what you're currently consuming. Let's take two examples: A, a 160-pound man who is eating too much—2,700 food calories plus 405 drink calories or 3,105 in all, and B, another 160-pound man who drinks too much—1,500 food calories plus 1,445 alcohol calories, or 2,945 in all. Both need to cut down to 2,400 calories daily, but A should cut only a drink or two from his regime and take the rest of the calories from his food intake, and B should keep on eating at his present rate and cut down on alcohol calories only.

Dieting while drinking: the limits

We've said before that the maximum number of alcohol calories the human organism can probably tolerate, nutritionally, is 40 percent of its daily intake (*tolerate,* not necessarily thrive on). The following table gives the number of drinks (or bottles of beer or glasses of wine) corresponding to 40 percent of the daily caloric requirement for various body weights. If you're *not* dieting, then your maximum is the figure for your present body weight. If you are dieting, drink up to the maximum for your *desired weight.*

Body weight	Maximum number of drinks
100 pounds	4
120 pounds	5
140 pounds	6
160 pounds	7
180 pounds	8
200 pounds	9
220 pounds	10
240 pounds	11

If you regularly drink more than your maximum, there is no way to handle the surplus calories, short of starving yourself, or taking up marathon running.

7

The Hangover

I feel as if midgets have been walking over my tongue with muddy feet.

—W. C. Fields

THE HEAD ACHES, the stomach is queasy, the limbs feel barely able to drag you around . . . you're hung over. What is a hangover, why do we get it, how can we cure or prevent it?

Some drinkers experience no hangover at all after a night of unusually heavy drinking. Others have only a mildly "not quite up to par" feeling. Still others experience excruciating torment. The symptoms of hangover vary from individual to individual, and they vary, also, according to how much you drink and how many years you've been drinking. A Finnish investigator, E. Tuominen, says that in early alcoholism, headaches, general indisposition and vomiting are the main hangover symptoms. Moderately advanced alcoholics exhibit tension, irritability, restlessness, stomach disturbances and guilt feelings. In long-standing, severe alcoholism, cardiac disturbances and psychotic symptoms are present. But what are the symptoms of hangover in the normal, nonalcoholic drinker? A Danish study lists 20:

Vomiting	Headache
Loss of appetite	Fatigue
Heartburn	Sweating
Lassitude	Disturbed balance, gait

Continued thirst	Tremor
Palpitation	Nystagmus (tremor of the eye-
Weakness of joints	balls)
Respiratory difficulties	General malaise
Sleeplessness	Anxiety
Giddiness	Depression
Pallor	

Basically, the hangover is a bunch of different reactions in the mind-body to the experience of having drunk "too much." Just what constitutes too much depends on the individual drinker. Of the people I interviewed, quantities of alcohol that would produce a hangover varied from "more than two glasses of wine" to "more than a fifth of whiskey." If averages mean anything, the average amount that is "too much" seems to be, for heavy drinkers, more than a pint of liquor and for more moderate drinkers, more than five or six drinks, during an evening's drinking.

Part of the cause of hangover is that some of the "too much" alcohol from last night is still swimming around in your veins. We drink more than we can oxidize during our night's sleep and wake up still partially drunk. Apparently heavy drinkers can tolerate some blood alcohol the next day. They can cope with drinking a pint, which at the rate of ½ ounce of alcohol per hour will take from thirteen to sixteen hours (depending on the proof of the liquor) to leave the body, but a pint and a half (nineteen to twenty-four hours' worth) produces hangover, a hangover that may just conveniently lift in time for the drinker to start his *next* drinking bout. Since moderate drinkers have hangovers on only six or eight hours' worth of alcohol, however, leftover alcohol is obviously not a cause of all hangovers. Let's look at some other factors.

Fatigue

Fatigue or lassitude in some form is part of every hangover. Frequently this is the effect of insufficient sleep: if you drink until 2 or 3 A.M. and then get up at 7:30 you can't expect to be in tiptop shape. But equally important is the quality of sleep you get. In recent years, studies of sleep have shown that there is a type of sleep called REM (rapid eye movement) sleep which is particularly important to the mental and physical well-being of the sleeper. When deprived of REM sleep, experimental subjects became irritable and anxious. Since in REM sleep the cortex or higher brain is very active, persons whose cortexes have been anesthetized by alcohol or sleeping pills cannot have REM sleep until the anesthesia wears off. So, if you go to bed sodden, the sleep you get for the next few hours will be unrestful and unrefreshing.

Another type of fatigue is due to the direct physiological effects of alcohol. We have seen how alcohol numbs the higher brain, masking its awareness of minor pain, fatigue or malaise. Failing to receive any signs of stress, the brain allows the body to overexert. (The phrase "roaring drunk" conjures up the extreme phase of alcoholic overexertion.) Even if the drinker does not stay out all night dancing or roaring about, his central nervous system is still out of control, allowing heartbeat, respiration and other functions to speed up without check. This overexertion produces a fatigue that is not felt at the time but is painfully obvious when the cortex wakes up.

Headache

The causes of the morning-after headache are not fully known. Perhaps there is not just one hangover headache. One type could be due to *vasodilation,* enlargement of the sensitive cranial arteries. Alcohol is a vasodilator, but since the headache does not occur at the time when alcohol is at a high level in the bloodstream, it is not directly caused by the alcohol but by fatigue, dehydration and other factors. Another kind of headache is the *muscle-contraction* or "tension" headache. This could be produced by sleeping with your head in an awkward posture for many hours. *Allergy* headaches could be produced by a sensitivity to the congeners in straight whiskey, or to substances such as tyramine—a central-nervous-system stimulant present in port, sherry and red table wines—or histamine, a vasodilator contained in significant amounts by certain red wines, particularly burgundies.

Caffeine, a vasoconstrictor, may help ease a headache due to vasodilation. Aspirin, a muscle relaxant, will subdue the tension headache. Take some of both, drink plenty of fluids, and if you can, go back to bed. . . .

Alcoholic "dehydration"

The extreme thirst sometimes felt during hangover is not caused by any real depletion of body fluids. True, alcohol does cause increased urination, but this is not sufficient to make for any significant drying-out of the body. What causes thirst is that the alcohol acts to alter the distribution of water in the body. Normally, about two-thirds of the water in the body is held within the cells. Alcohol causes this balance to change, decreasing the amount of fluid in the cells and increasing extracellular fluids. The body as a whole has lost no water, but the cells are feeling parched. Hence your thirst.

Nausea, vomiting, heartburn

Drinking too much strong liquor is a shock (or "insult," as doctors like to call it) to the digestive system. For a neophyte drinker, two or three drinks are sufficient insult to cause his stomach to rebel. A fairly experienced drinker may require a pint or more to bring him to the same state. The habitual heavy drinker's stomach, like the old dray horse that has become inured to the whip, has learned that it's useless to try to fight off the booze and so does not. Vomiting during or right after drinking usually occurs only with relatively inexperienced or nontolerant drinkers.

Morning-after vomiting, however, can happen to the most

habituated. The digestive system was able to cope with the overload of liquor it was given last night, but now it rejects any further contributions. The hungover drinker swallows his breakfast orange juice and suddenly it's as if he had swallowed a depth charge. The stomach rumbles and erupts. Will accept no more nourishment until many hours have passed. Finally the crisis passes and digestion is back to normal—until the next overload. Alcoholic irritation of the mucous lining of the digestive tract ("heartburn") is often present, and in some drinkers becomes chronic, so that vomiting and discomfort are frequent. This is a serious problem in that the sufferer tends no longer to eat well; the resulting nutritional deficiencies further aggravate the gastritis and also impair the digestive process so that vitamins and other nutrients are poorly absorbed. At this point a sojourn on the wagon is indicated plus, probably, injections of the B vitamins. Chronic gastritis should be treated by a physician.

Remorse and emotional pain

The most excruciating hangover seems to be the one in which the sufferer wakes up and thinks something like, *"Oh, I've done it again! I got drunk last night and now I'm being punished good and proper. What a miserable, rotten wretch I am!"* This phenomenon is common in alcoholics. As Dr. Benjamin Karpman says in his book *The Hangover,* "The increasing misery of the hangover is not due to the headache, the nausea, the cold sweats, the chills and fever, or even the shakes, but to the emotional pain that accompanies them—the guilt, anxiety, self-accusation, the sense of hopelessness and despair." These feelings occur with social drinkers too. We probably all know at least one drinker who goes through a hangover doubled over in misery and swearing never, never, never to drink that much again.

One friend of mine who was drinking rather heavily and

coming to work late, hung over and remorseful every morning, got fired from his job. "I didn't so much mind his coming in late," his boss reported. "What I couldn't stand were those constant apologies."

Perhaps some of these drinkers are overdramatizing the whole ritual of drinking and take perverse pride in how drunk they get at night and how terribly they suffer the next morning. Others may have genuine emotional conflicts about drinking (or their behavior *while* drinking) which cause them to amplify the pain signals of hangover as a sort of punishment or atonement. Another group may be suffering emotionally because of vitamin depletion. (A number of drinkers have told me their morning-after depression goes away when they take 100 to 400 mg. of niacinamide.) In any case, the *worst* hangover is the one in which emotional distress predominates.

IS there a hangover cure?

Unfortunately, the hangover has not been the object of much medical research. Delirium tremens, which might be considered a super-hangover, responds nicely to adrenal steroids (ACTH), but using such powerful medication on the ordinary hangover would be totally unsound—no doctor would prescribe it.

One possible hangover cure (or preventive) has been identified, but it is not at present available in this country. The substance in question is called *pyritinol* (trade name Encephabol, manufactured by E. Merck & Co., Darmstadt, West Germany). It is related to but not chemically the same as vitamin B_6, pyridoxine. Since a number of studies had indicated that pyritinol had a protective effect in animals against the symptoms of alcohol intoxication, a group of Danish researchers decided to try the substance in experiments with humans. Using a group of volunteers, they made a double-blind experiment in which the participants were invited to a series of parties where they were encouraged to drink, talk, sing and dance. One half the group were given placebos, the other half 1,200 mg. of pyritinol in three doses: 400 mg. at the beginning of the party, 400 three hours later, and 400 at the end of the party. The next morning the subjects were visited at their places of work, given a check list of hangover symptoms, and asked to mark those symptoms, if any, they thought were most applicable to their condition. At a subsequent party the roles were reversed: subjects who had received pyritinol received placebos, and vice versa.

The results of the experiment were highly significant. The subjects *not* receiving pyritinol reported over 50 percent more hangover symptoms than those who did get the drug. In addition, three participants, after placebo, had total amnesia with regard to what happened at the party, whereas after pyritinol they had no such experience. Some of the subjects who drank the most during the parties exhibited slurred speech during the placebo session but not with pyritinol. The drug is not at present licensed by the FDA for import or use in this country and no U.S. studies have been made. One would hope, however, that such a promising initial report would be followed up by *somebody*. . . .

How about a hair of the dog that bit you?

Alcohol works tolerably well as a *temporary* abater of hangovers. If you drink enough to reach Stage One or Stage Two, you may succeed in masking your fatigue and some other minor symptoms. (Taking the booze in a Bloody Mary or other highly spiced drink will help mask gastric distress, much as liniment masks muscle aches.) But in so doing you may not get the rest you need and may find, particularly if you slide into Stage Three or beyond, that next day's hangover is even worse. If you must fight booze with booze, do so only occasionally. Habitual use of more drink to cure hangovers could put you in the same bind as the terminal drunk: he *must* drink, because only alcohol can make him feel better.

Vitamins can help . . . a little

Since vitamin deficiencies play so enormous a part in what goes wrong with drinkers, one might expect that taking vitamins would help a hangover. And so it does, for some people. The vitamins most likely to help are the water-soluble ones, B-complex and C, and the minerals. Fat-soluble vitamins such as A, D and E may indeed be also deficient, but there's little chance that taking them would have any results during the period of the hangover, since they go to work more slowly.

A couple of years ago, for instance, I was having severe hangovers—no headache or nausea, but pronounced fatigue plus a highly unsettling internal queasiness or shakiness. I decided to experiment with vitamins and see if I could relieve my symptoms. I began with the B vitamins, taking a high-potency B-complex capsule plus large extra doses of B_1, B_2, B_6 and niacinamide. Though I could feel, taste and smell surplus B vitamins exuding from every pore, my hangover remained the same. Then I tried vitamin C—about 2,000 milligrams dissolved in water. There was an immediate result, but not an especially dramatic one: I felt somewhat refreshed and less worn out though the hangover was still unpleasant. The mitigating effects of the C alone were minimal, however. Then one day it occurred to me I might be deficient in magnesium. Magnesium deficiency can cause nervous and muscular irritability, muscle cramps and spasms, convulsions, and probably is an important factor in causing delirium tremens. I took a teaspoon of Epsom salt (magnesium sulfate) dissolved in water and got almost immediate relief from the queasy, shaky feelings that had been bothering me. I've had hangovers since but never severe ones.

Other people have reported to me that their hangovers *are* helped by B vitamins—B_1, niacinamide and B_6 in particular.

The point is that for vitamins to be of any effect *there must be a deficiency.* If you're already a health-food-and-vitamin "true believer," you're probably wasting time and money trying to cure your hangovers with more vitamins.

If you want to try vitamins on your next hangover, here's a dosage that might show results.

One high-potency multivitamin, multimineral capsule plus:

100 mg. B_1
100 mg. B_2
100 mg. B_6
400 mg. niacinamide
2,000 mg. vitamin C
Enough *dolomite* (calcium-magnesium supplement) to provide 1,000 mg. calcium

Should there be no beneficial effect after several trials, forget about morning-after vitamin therapy, although you may indeed have vitamin shortages (see Chapter 5).

The only *sure* cure for hangover is the traditional one: drink plenty of fluids; eat bland, soothing foods; get lots of rest . . . and *be patient!*

Preventing the hangover

It's a lot easier to avoid a hangover than it is to cure one. Here's a surefire method of never having hangovers—providing you're able to follow all the suggestions.

1. Eat before drinking, preferably rather fatty foods. Alcohol has an affinity with fat, and fat retards alcohol absorption more than other foods.

2. Drink less, if you possibly can.

3. After drinking, don't go right to sleep. Stay up for two or more hours. Drink lots of fluids, have a few cups of coffee, eat something. If you're headachy, take two aspirin before going to bed.

4. Sleep late.

5. Be complacent, rather than guilty, about your drinking.

8

Alcohol and Sex

THE CONVENTIONAL VIEW of the relationship between alcohol and sex is still that expressed by the porter in *Macbeth*. Speaking of drink he says, "Lechery, sir, it provokes, and unprovokes: it provokes the desire, but it takes away the performance." Is this picture of the horny but incapable drinker a true one? Not really.

In his book *Executive Life-Styles*, a study of the sexual and drinking habits of six thousand executives, Dr. Harry Johnson reports that the heaviest drinkers are also the most sexually active. Dr. Johnson's figures confirm the first of Shakespeare's statements: drink *does* provoke lechery. Of the men who drank only occasionally, 18.9 percent found liquor sexually stimulating. Of those who took two to four drinks a day, 51 percent reported that drinking excited them sexually. And 60.9 percent of the men who drank more than four drinks a day experienced the same effect.

Heavier drinking leads to heavier sex, according to the survey. The percentage of men in Dr. Johnson's most-active category (those having intercourse more than twice a week) increased with their alcohol consumption:

Daily alcohol consumption	*Percentage of men having intercourse more than twice weekly*
None	17.3
Under 2 oz.	17.9

2–4 oz.	18.7
4–6 oz.	21.1
Over 6 oz.	27.9

The same survey found that the executive's alcohol consumption rises with his salary; the highest income group was also the hardest-drinking. So we could say that—in the business world, at least—the American male who is the *most* sexually active is the one who makes over $50,000 a year and is also a heavy drinker.

In interviews with 43 drinkers, 24 men and 19 women, I asked how alcohol affected their sex lives. Of the men, 3 reported that drinking takes away performance (for days after a drinking bout, said one man); 4 found drinking a deterrent to sex and said that it made sex unappealing or unesthetic; 2 reported that drinking slowed their orgasms too much, so that their partners became worn out; and 15 said that drinking made them more active sexually. Of the women, 2 reported that although drinking made them more amorous and adventurous it also inhibited performance; 3 said drinking made "no difference"; and 14 felt that drinking improved and enhanced sex.

Some comments by my interviewees:

Women
It makes me more amorous, definitely.

I get more creative in bed, better able to express myself.

Sex drunk is different from sex sober. I get more lively and versatile, try things that I wouldn't ordinarily.

It relaxes me and makes me feel more open to the experience.

If anything, it makes me more horny.

I get more adventurous but I don't go through with it. I'd like to go looking for adventure but then I have a personality change that gets in the way before anything happens.

Men

Drinking on sex life is negative. I mean sex has to have a degree of sensitivity to it, so neither one of you can be loaded. There's no fun screwing a drunken broad, even if she's your wife.

Liquor is a turn-on. Get stoned enough and you're practically a walking Id. And when Id meets Id, watch out. Sober, I'll see a pretty girl across the room and feel a twinge of lust which I do nothing about. Stoned, I may easily walk right over and start necking with her.

It releases my inhibitions and turns me into a more sexual person. Without drinks, my tendency would be to come too fast and be a dissatisfying mate in that respect. Liquor slows down the response there. It's definitely congenial to good sexual relationships.

A little bit of it helps as a relaxant, I think. But there's a communications thing that ought to happen and if either party or both overdrink, the quality of the communication suffers.

It depends on how sexual and raunchy you want to be. Before I was married I'd spend whole weekends with various girlfriends just drinking and fucking, fucking and drinking. Without the liquor it would be more like wham-bam-thank-you-m'am and now-let's-go-look-at-the-beautiful-sunrise. If you want to be carnal all the way you need the drinking.

But alcohol CAN inhibit sex

One of the effects of cirrhosis of the liver is impotence, usually irreversible even if the patient stops drinking and recovers from the cirrhosis. Some noncirrhotic drinkers apparently suffer a milder version of this. Through excessive drinking their liver becomes impaired and is no longer able to suppress excessive estrogen ("female" hormone) in the system. The rising estrogen level causes the sex drive to diminish, and eventually would cause the sufferer to become feminized (grow breasts, lose body hair, etc.)

One of my subjects, a man in his middle forties, reported

going through this experience. He was drinking quite heavily and having frequent intercourse with both his wife and his mistress. Then one day he realized that satisfying his two ladies was becoming a chore rather than a pleasure. He had little desire for sex and would perform, perfunctorily, only when his partner insisted. "It was as if my sex desire was just draining away," he told me. He consulted his doctor, who diagnosed the condition as being due to defective liver function. The doctor advised a drastic reduction in the man's liquor intake plus vitamin B_1 therapy, 50 mg. three times a day. After several weeks on this regime, the man's libido returned full blast.

Is alcohol an aphrodisiac?

The answer to that question would be a qualified "yes." For people who feel they are inhibited or too "civilized" to get the most out of sex or who prize the coarser, more physical and instinctual forms of sexuality, liquor does act to enhance sexual desire and performance. For others, to whom the drunken state seems unattractive, it will have the reverse effect.

9

The Myth of
the Drunken Driver

THE REMARKABLE THING about drunken drivers is not that many of them get into crashes, but that so many do not. Drunk driving is a much-studied subject, and the statistics compiled on it would reach from here to Jupiter and back if strung out sheet by sheet. We know, for instance, that between 10 percent and 20 percent of all drivers on the road at any given moment will have alcohol in their veins. From 1 to 3 percent will have enough to make them legally drunk. If one considers only nighttime drivers, of course, the figure would be higher. Now interpolate another set of figures: of the 14 million-odd routine crashes that occur in the nation every year, about 6 percent involve a drunken driver. Fooling around with these figures a bit, one comes up with the information that of every million drunk drivers on the road, 999,600 will arrive home safely.

The average drunk, in other words, has about a 3,000 to 1 chance of *not* having an accident when he drives. These figures are approximate, of course, as are most attempts to make sense out of statistics.

A more troubling report is that drunken drivers are involved in a high percentage of all the *fatal* crashes in this country. Just how high no one seems to know. One researcher who has given the matter a great deal of attention, Richard Zylman of the

Center for Alcohol Studies at Rutgers, says that much of the data we are given on alcohol and driving is misquoted, inconsistent, misinterpreted or simply unsubstantiated. Instead of 50 to 85 percent of fatal accidents being caused by drunk drivers, as one often reads, Zylman estimates the correct figure to be 43 percent. That's still a lot. Why, when the role of the drunk driver is relatively minor in ordinary crashes, is it so enormous in the fatal ones? A prominent safety-research scientist, W. L. Carlson, puts much of it down to "inexperience with drinking-and-driving." With male drivers the peak year for fatal crashes *not* involving alcohol is eighteen, or shortly after learning to drive. Peak year for alcohol-involved fatal crashes is twenty-one, an age at which most young men are still rather new to alcohol. Women do not have "danger years" as do men, a fact well known to insurance actuaries, and compared with males there are very few female drunks on the roads (at least behind the wheel). When a woman driver does drink, however, she is more likely than the male to have a crash, even at the relatively low blood-alcohol concentration of .05 percent. Carlson regards this fact, also, as an instance of inexperience with drinking-and-driving.

As usual, when there's any sort of choice to be made between truthfulness, accuracy and social effectiveness on the one hand and anti-alcohol zeal on the other, anti-alcohol zeal gets the nod. An enormous amount of road-safety propaganda for the last several decades has been devoted to giving the public the impression that the No. 1 menace on our highways is the drunken driver. Even leaving aside the fact that in the main only *young* drunks are menaces, the plain fact is that while 43 percent of fatal crashes, or whatever figure is correct, are caused by drunks, 100 percent are caused by *drivers.* Drinking is almost impossible to control or police. Driving is not—we could simply make driver's licenses harder to get and easier to lose.

This, of course, strikes at a right every American considers even more basic than the right to bear arms—the right to own and operate an automobile. To lose one's driver's license is to become a second-class citizen, and where they have any discretion the courts are notoriously reluctant to inflict such a punishment, even on drunks. I once knew a blind man who was allowed to keep his driver's license. Asked if it was not illegal for Charlie to be driving, the town clerk said, "Well, sure it's illegal, but I mean, the poor fellow's got to get around, don't he?" In return for being forgiven an eye examination, Charlie had to promise to use his car on one route only, between his house and the beginning of Main Street, and back. To be sure, he wasn't totally blind—he could tell the difference between light and dark quite well and sometimes recognize large objects by their outline. He never ran over anything larger than a dog or chicken.

If we were really concerned with cutting down highway fatalities, we would make every driver pass a really tough test for skill in driving, quick reflexes and good judgment before awarding him a license, and we'd yank that license away again at the slightest hint of any pattern of recklessness or disregard for the law, including the laws against drinking and driving. But we're *not* concerned with fatalities or crashes. They're part of the pageant of life in America. So, instead of doing something to enforce traffic safety, we make a fuss about drunks. We're not even really concerned about *them*—imagine the dismay if everyone followed the injunction not to mix drinking and driving. Such a clutter of abandoned cars! Gasoline pumps lying idle! They might even have to postpone the next oil crisis!

Although the fact will never be legally recognized, there is such a thing as a safe drunken driver. I've known many. Two were cabdrivers out in San Francisco, where I once had a job driving a cab on the night shift. One was a gentleman in his sixties who'd been a drunk for forty years and a cabdriver for the same amount of time. Frank always drove around with a "mickey" (half pint) in his coat pocket and two or three more under the front seat. He felt that buying a larger-size bottle than that was a sign of intemperance if not degeneracy. He sometimes was too drunk to get up out of his seat but never too drunk to drive. His colleague was a much younger man, fat, pleasant-faced and smiling, yet with a certain dreamy, faraway quality to him. You'd be faraway too if you consumed as many screwdrivers per shift as Al did. He took his provisions aboard in two quart bottles of Tropicana; half of the contents of each had been poured off and replaced with 100-proof Smirnoff. Once in a while Al would chuckle and say, "Orange juice is good for you." Neither of these men had ever had any serious accident, nor did anyone complain about their driving. Frank had a tendency to be irascible with passengers, though. (I can see now that it was just his polyneuritis acting up.)

Another fine drunk driver is a well-known author, one of the ornaments of our contemporary literature. I've been a guest in this man's car three times now. Each time he was thoroughly polluted yet drove with impressive smoothness and aplomb— one felt instinctively safe in his hands. I'd rather ride with him than two-thirds of the hackies in New York.

The fact that alcohol does not necessarily impair skill and coordination was confirmed in the laboratory in an experiment conducted at Harvard Medical School by Dr. Jack Mendelson and his associates. As the experimenters say in their report:

> It is widely believed that ability to drive a car begins to be impaired at a blood alcohol level of about 50 mg. per 100 ml., and that people who regularly drink a great deal do not have very different threshold levels from those who drink very little. But there is experimental evidence for the opposite view, that heavy drinkers show fewer behavioral signs of intoxication, or show them at higher blood alcohol levels than do light drinkers.
>
> We know of no previous study in which motor skills were tested under alcohol doses as large and prolonged over time as in the present experiment. Our prediction was that a total daily dose of 30 oz. of whisky would reliably slow down responses, disrupt coordinated movements, and increase errors in tasks involving choice

and decision. We administered three tests of motor performance which . . . probe three more or less independent abilities in the normal population. One test measured the speed of initiating responses; a second assessed the rate at which continuous simple manual performance is sustained; a third probed a more complex motor skill. Two of these tests also allowed for a controlled variation of the level of task complexity.

A group of chronic heavy drinkers were the subjects. During the first two weeks they were given daily doses of 30 ounces of whiskey. This amount of booze had no adverse effect on their speed or skill, except that they performed most efficiently after consuming a moderate amount of their daily allotment, slightly better than before drinking at all or after drinking the whole 30 ounces. This is typical of the heavy drinker—he's more "himself" with a few drinks under his belt. Only when the whiskey ration was increased to 40 ounces daily did the testees show any impairment of skill.

From a socio-ethical rather than a legal point of view, the real crime is to drive a car on the public thoroughfares when you're not competent to operate it properly. Being a sober bad driver doesn't make you any less guilty.

10

Who or What Is an Alcoholic?

I'm sorry, but you've contracted that dreaded of all diseases, mogo on the gogogo.

—W. C. Fields

MANY DRINKERS TEND to worry about whether or not they are alcoholics, or incipient or borderline alcoholics, or in danger of becoming so. So let's go into this question.

Is an alcoholic someone who often staggers when he walks? Someone with a lot of empty whiskey bottles on his back porch? Someone who drinks more than a certain amount? Someone who likes to drink alone, or in the morning? Someone who's often late to work because of being hung over? Someone who acts weird or goes berserk after a couple of drinks? Someone who always gets blotto at parties?

What *is* an alcoholic, anyway?

Consider: George and Muriel like to drink and in fact they drink a whole lot. Martinis begin flowing as soon as George gets home from work, wine or more drinks are served at dinner, and after dinner the couple continue to imbibe until falling-down drunk. Often they have guests, friends who drink just as heartily as they do. At work, George often brags about what a monumental hangover he has, and everyone chuckles sympathetically. George works in an occupation which looks favorably upon liquor. If once in a while he happens to get spifflicated at lunch, his boss and colleagues are quite understanding—after all, it could, and does, happen to them also. Muriel gets her children off to school on time every morning, keeps her house clean and tidy, and in general is regarded as a model member of the community. In fact, she was chairman of the PTA last year and is a leading light in the local ecology movement. Are George and Muriel alcoholics? Not to themselves, their friends, George's employers, or the community at large. True, there are people who would regard them as alcoholics, but those people are not part of George and Muriel's crowd.

Sidney drinks less than George does, but his wife, Lucille, and most of their friends are teetotalers. Lucille had an uncle who was "taken by the booze" and has hated alcohol ever since. When Sidney exhibits signs of drunkenness at family gatherings, Lucille is deeply ashamed and everyone else looks the other way, trying to ignore the disgrace of it all. Sidney feels quite guilty after one of these episodes. Twice in the last ten years, Lucille has had him committed briefly as an alcoholic and once she had him arrested, when he slapped her during a marital argument.

Although Sidney's boss has no strong opinions, pro or con, about drinking, he has heard of all this and watches his employee closely for signs of his going "out of control." Sidney does his job perhaps a little better than George does his, but he will never be promoted to a key position in his company. To his wife, his friends, his employer, even to himself, Sidney *is* an alcoholic.

"Alcoholism" is an example of what the eminent sociologist Erving Goffman calls "the insanity of place." We might call it *inappropriate* drunkenness. Someone who shows up drunk in church, or in the courtroom, is *out of place,* whereas someone drunk at a cocktail party is usually not. A perfect case of insanity of place was reported in the newspapers recently. One

Robert Friedman, of Chicago, was arrested for panhandling in front of a downtown bus station. Friedman, a frugal, miserly type, was carrying a briefcase containing $24,087 in small bills. A few days later the judge committed him to a mental institution, where he still remains at this writing. Friedman's lawyer says he fears that his client's case is a "frighteningly common one" of persons ordered to spend the rest of their lives unheard from because they are eccentric, though sane. "His only obsession in life was saving money, unfortunately. If he hadn't had that money when he was panhandling, he'd be a free man today."

So we have a sociological definition of alcoholism: An "alcoholic" is someone who while drinking, or *by* drinking, *breaks social rules* or *fails to adhere to social rituals* generally accepted in his milieu.

What about medical definitions?

No one can deny that there are many sick people who drink and many people who have made themselves sick by drinking. But is there any such thing as a progressive disease *of* drinking, brought about *by* drinking, called *alcoholism*? No, not in any definition that makes sense. I invite any reader who doubts this statement to read a book called *The Disease Concept of Alcoholism,* by E. M. Jellinek. Meticulously researched and presented with admirable fairness, the book reviews virtually all the arguments ever made pro and con the disease concept of alcoholism and all the explanations or "etiologies" suggested for such a disease, none of which are entirely convincing or satisfactory to the author. The one argument that he does find convincing is as follows. After acknowledging that there is no clear-cut definition of the term "disease," Dr. Jellinek goes on:

> Pointing out this lack of definition of disease by no means involves a reproach. The splendid progress of medicine shows that this branch of the sciences can function extremely well without

such a definition. Physicians know what belongs in their realm.

It comes to this, that *a disease is what the medical profession recognizes as such.* The fact that they are not able to explain the nature of such a condition does not constitute proof that it is not an illness. There are many instances in the history of medicine of diseases whose nature was unknown for many years. The nature of some is still unknown, but they are nevertheless unquestionable medical problems.

. . . the medical profession has officially accepted alcoholism as an illness, and through this fact alone alcoholism becomes an illness, whether a part of the lay public likes it or not, and even if a minority of the medical profession is disinclined to accept the idea.

Rather a saber-rattling statement, don't you think? Though of course absurd from a scientific point of view, it makes perfect *political* sense. Legally, there *is* such a thing as alcoholism, and physicians are empowered to diagnose this condition and if necessary have the sufferer forcibly committed for treatment.

Elsewhere in his book, Dr. Jellinek gives an all-purpose definition of alcoholism: *any use of alcoholic beverages that causes any damage to the individual or society or both.* He makes the statement deliberately vague, so as to encompass all possible notions of alcoholism. In this country, for instance, the generally-accepted version of an alcoholic is someone who craves liquor and who, once he's taken one drink, cannot stop until he's totally blotto. Some "students" of American alcoholism, however, would include under the term heavy weekend drinkers as well as "relief drinkers" who never become "addicted." In France, the heaviest-drinking nation in the world, there is little overt drunkenness of the Stage Three or Stage Four variety. Instead, the average Frenchman consumes from two to three liters of wine throughout the day, maintaining a state in which he is never really drunk, yet is never quite sober. Without ever showing much drunkenness, French alcoholics do contract all the classic alcoholic ills—delirium tremens, cirrhosis, Wernicke's syndrome, and so on. The French alcoholic is said to be *alcoolisé*—alcoholized. In Finland, where the sale of liquor is restricted to the large cities, alcoholism takes the form of men coming into town, having a few drinks, and becoming violent—"explosive drinking." In Italy, any sign of drunkenness whatever is considered a violation of social rules, except in the coarsest of circles—an alcoholic is anyone who cannot hold his liquor or who shows signs of being in Stage Two or beyond.

Let's try another definition: *The word "alcoholic" is a vague term used to disparage someone who drinks.*

Take someone who likes to drink, spends a little more time than he ought to on liquor, sometimes shows up late to work due to a hangover or doesn't come in at all, and occasionally has arguments with friends or family while somewhat smashed. How does one redefine him as an alcoholic? By disparaging his motives and actions and emphasizing the "damage" he causes. Here is how Dr. Jellinek goes about the task (italics mine):

> Alpha alcoholism represents a purely psychological *continual dependence or reliance* upon the effect of alcohol to *relieve bodily or emotional pain.* The drinking is *"undisciplined"* in the sense that it *contravenes such rules as society tacitly agrees upon*—such as time, locale, amount and effect of drinking—but does not lead to "loss of control" or "inability to abstain." The *damage* caused by this species of alcoholism may be restricted to the *disturbance of interpersonal relations.* There may also be *interference with the family budget,* occasional *absenteeism from work* and *decreased productivity,* and some of the *nutritional deficiencies of alcoholism,* but not the disturbances due to withdrawal from alcohol. Nor are there any signs of a progressive process.

Again: Who or what is an alcoholic?

The facts of drinking are relatively straightforward. Increased or prolonged drinking leads to increased tolerance for alcohol, allowing the drinker to drink more and function more effectively in the drunken state than he initially could. Increased tolerance also leads to loss of control over one's drinking, since in the successive stages of drunkenness the drinker is unable to maintain sober or "conscious" control. In addition, drinking in the absence of proper nutrition produces multiple ills which may become quite severe, even fatal, and may induce discomfort which only further drinking can relieve. Furthermore, prolonged or excessive drinking of alcohol may produce possibly irreversible tissue damage. While we don't know everything about alcohol, certainly more is known about its effects and side effects than is known of many other drugs and medications in common use.

Given the present state of knowledge, it ought to be possible to diagnose and treat the various ills attendant on drinking in a sensible, rational way.

But we're not rational about alcohol. There is always that whiff of brimstone, *frisson* of terror, hint of degradation, twinge of revulsion or pious desire to save someone from himself that occurs when the notion "alcoholic" enters in. Society is itself irrational and has always responded better to myths than realities—whether these are "good" myths like George Washington and the cherry tree or "bad" ones like the Germans impaling babies on their bayonets in World War I. As examples of alcoholism, Ray Milland's bender in *The Lost Weekend* or Tyrone Power's descent into geekdom in *Nightmare Alley* are more real to us than anything that actually happens.

The whole business reminds one of the story about the little boy who had a phobia about *kreplach* (a wonton-like Jewish dumpling). In an effort to persuade the boy his fears were silly, the psychiatrist took him into his mother's kitchen and showed him a square of *kreplach* dough. "Does this frighten you?" he asked. The little boy shook his head. The psychiatrist said, "Now I'm going to fold over one corner of the dough, like this. Are you frightened?" Again the boy shook his head. The second corner was folded over. No fright. The third. No reaction. But when the psychiatrist folded over the fourth corner, the boy recoiled in horror and with a cry of "Arrrgghh, *kreplach!*" fled the room.

Similarly, we cry "alcoholic" when the symptoms observed fit our own private picture of that condition. For one person the sight of a whiskey bottle sticking out of someone's pocket might be enough, while another might need to see a derelict passed out in a doorway or having DTs in a hospital ward.

In the absence of any agreed-upon definition, it would seem that there are only three ways one could properly use the term "alcoholic." An alcoholic is:

1. Anyone who drinks at all. This is fine, but it would of course include everybody from the priest who sips the communion wine to terminal drunks.

2. Anyone who is *thought* to be alcoholic by anyone else. Rather silly, but closest to current usage.

3. Anyone who calls himself an alcoholic.

The third would seem to be the fairest use of the term. It is impossible to know what's going on in the head of your fellow man unless he tells you. For instance, a man enters his house on a Friday evening with an armload of bottles, drinks all weekend and emerges Monday morning, unshaven, trembly and bleary-eyed, saying, "Boy, did I tie one on this weekend! Enjoyed every minute of it! Terrific!" Okay, he may be a jerk, but he's no alcoholic. But if the same fellow came off his bender moaning, "Oh, my God, how could I do such an awful thing! I'm a sick man, help me," then he's a legitimate self-admitted alcoholic and good luck to him.

The role of guilt and fear

Since this book is aimed at the normal social drinker rather than the alcoholic or "problem drinker," I've made no attempt to seek out people who felt they had drinking problems. I did encounter some, however, and in talking to them I was struck by a certain pattern of self-doubt and self-castigation that cropped up in all their conversations. "Drinking's a filthy habit," one man told me. "I don't know why I do it. I become disgusting when I drink, just like a beast. [Something I've failed to observe, though I've seen him drunk.] I was much better off when I was on the wagon."

I talked with a girl in her early twenties who feels she has a drinking problem because she has had blackouts after drinking and while drunk has made phone calls and written letters that were bolder and/or more hostile than she liked to think about when sober. This girl's parents had both been alcoholics, and she had a deep fear of ending up "like them."

Another man told me, "I have self-destructive tendencies, I know that. That's what my drinking is all about. I just hope I don't end up in Bellevue or on the Bowery someday." This was a prosperous advertising executive whose drinking seems to an outsider unexceptional and well controlled.

Self-doubt, ambivalence and guilt feelings about drinking, and a fear of alcoholism seem to be universal among people who feel they have a drinking problem. There are members of Alcoholics Anonymous who joined in their teens or early twenties after a very limited drinking experience and have remained members ever since. What drinking they did threw a scare into them from which they have not recovered. Some people don't even need to drink at all to arrive at a similar conclusion. I've heard several nondrinkers say that the reason they don't touch alcohol is that "I just know I'd turn into an alcoholic if I did."

Three of the normal drinkers I interviewed—two men and one woman, all in their forties—told me that at one point in their lives they had become worried that their drinking was turning into alcoholism and had joined AA. Later they decided their worries were baseless and went back to drinking again.

Helping the alcoholic

If we accept the notion that an alcoholic is someone who acknowledges (or imagines) that he is drinking in a self-destructive way, we still are faced with the problem of what to do for him. The traditional approach—treating alcoholism as a unitary process or disease caused by drinking—has the defect that it *blames drinking* for the alcoholic's plight and by so doing lumps together two factors that don't necessarily belong together. The physical and mental effects of excessive drinking are well known and can usually be cured and/or prevented by vitamin-mineral therapy plus adequate nutrition. But the other factor in alcoholism—the desire to drink self-destructively (or to fancy that one does)—is not inevitably connected to alcohol. Alcohol addicts could just as easily choose narcotics or barbiturates (many have at one time or another) to be the focus of their addiction—or gambling, or overeating. The alcoholic is an addictive personality, someone with an urge to be dependent, and alcohol just happens to be the substance he has chosen for his dependency. Alcohol itself does not cause dependency. Let me quote from the book *Love and Addiction,* by Stanton Peele and Archie Brodsky:

> Addiction is not a chemical reaction. Addiction is an *experience,* one which grows out of an individual's routinized subjective response to something that has special meaning for him—something, anything, that he finds so safe and reassuring that he cannot be without it. So if we want to come to terms with addiction, we have to stop pointing the finger at drugs and start looking at people, at ourselves, and at what makes us dependent. We will find that we learn habits of dependence in part by growing up in a culture which teaches a sense of personal inadequacy, a reliance on external bulwarks, and a preoccupation with the negative or painful rather than the positive or joyous.
>
> Our customary image of the dirty, despised "drug addict" or alcoholic is part of a general conception of addiction as an abnormality of our society. But in reality, addiction is not an aberration from the norm; it is itself the norm. Drug dependency is a mirror-image of more basic dependencies that we learn at home and in school. The addict's search for a hollow, external resolution of life

(whether through a drug or an escapist love affair) follows directly from the hollow, external relationships we are led to have with each other, with our minds and bodies, with the physical world, with learning and work and play. Those young people who suddenly repudiate convention and seek some ultimate solace in acid or speed, or a religious commune, are only expressing tendencies that were always present in the accepted guise of a superficial home and school life.

Medical science has the answer—a relatively simple one—to the side effects of excessive drinking. Let it not also pretend it knows how to cure the desire to be dependent. That is something that only a spontaneous change of heart by the addict himself can accomplish.

11

Health Hazards of Drinking

THERE IS NO QUESTION that the heavy and/or prolonged drinking of alcohol can be a threat to health and, ultimately, to life itself. So, in varying degrees, are smoking, lack of exercise, obesity and lack of proper nutrition. Psychologically negative conditions such as general unhappiness, depression, tension, anxiety, chronic rage and frustration (sexual or otherwise) can contribute to the hazard also. The more these other conditions are present together with alcohol, the greater the threat to health and life span.

It has been estimated that excessive drinking removes ten to twenty years from the normal life expectancy. Empirically, this estimate seems more or less correct, if one looks at all the drinkers who die in their sixth decade (or before) rather than in the seventh or eighth. The famous publisher Joseph Pulitzer, a two-quart-a-day man who liked to direct the affairs of his newspaper empire from the privacy of his yacht so that no one could see him drunk, lived to be sixty-four. John Barrymore, a very heavy drinker, died of cirrhosis in 1942 at the age of sixty —by contrast his brother Lionel, though crippled, survived until seventy-six and sister Ethel to eighty. W. C. Fields, a man of exceptionally rugged constitution, died at sixty-six of cirrhosis complicated by heart trouble. For every Winston Churchill who lives into ripe old age despite a heavy alcohol habit, there would appear to be thousands of others whose drinking shortens their lives.

Thus, unless you sincerely consider dying of the drink a glorious way to go (which it isn't, especially toward the end), it would be well to think of cutting down to a sensible intake sometime during the fourth decade of your life, or most certainly the fifth. Frequent checkups by a doctor, preferably one who's had a lot of experience with the health problems of drinkers, are also indicated.

Let's look at some of the health hazards drinkers may encounter.

Alcohol and Your Liver

The liver is the largest gland in the body, a complex chemical factory which serves as a source of fuel for the organism, a waste-disposal system removing toxins and impurities from the blood, a manufacturer of hormones and enzymes, and has many other functions besides. The liver is a busy organ. It converts starch into glycogen, then stores it, releasing the glycogen for energy as is needed. It breaks down protein into amino acids, stores fat and vitamins, destroys and recycles old blood cells, releases antibodies into the bloodstream . . . and handles the metabolism of alcohol.

The average adult liver weighs about four pounds and is located in the right upper abdomen, directly below the diaphragm. In a healthy state, it does not protrude beneath the ribs. Under the influence of too much alcohol, however, it can increase enormously in size, sometimes virtually filling the right side of the abdomen. One of the admirable characteristics of the liver is its reserve capacity. As much as two-thirds of its cells can be destroyed yet the remainder will carry out all the required functions. The liver also has amazing powers of regeneration. Given a rest of a few days or weeks from whatever poison has been destroying it—in our case alcohol—it will grow back to its former size and efficiency.

The primary effect of alcohol is to produce *fatty liver*. This is not a long-drawn-out process, but occurs instantly on ingestion of alcohol. The liver stops burning its normal fuel, fat, and switches to the alcohol instead. Ingesting just one martini will raise the fat content of the liver from a normal 3 percent to about 3½. Further drinks will increase fat content accordingly. One need not be an alcoholic or heavy drinker to develop fatty liver—regular moderate drinkers have it also. Fatty liver is not a disease in itself, simply a condition which may or may not lead to health-threatening complications.

No causal relationship between fatty liver and actual liver diseases such as *alcoholic hepatitis* and *cirrhosis* has been demonstrated. Although heavy drinking almost invariably deposits excess fat in the liver, only a tiny minority of heavy drinkers develop cirrhosis. It is therefore thought that moderate or intermittent fatty liver probably does not in itself lead to cirrhosis. Since cirrhosis is definitely associated with prolonged heavy drinking, however, it is likely that the burden placed on the organ by *extreme* fattiness, plus perhaps other factors not presently known, does bring about the disease. The whole process is not yet well understood.

Alcoholic hepatitis is an inflammation of the liver brought about by excessive drinking, usually over a period of years, plus probably a deficiency of protein and vitamins in the diet. (An adequate protein intake tends to protect the liver from damage by alcohol.) The symptoms of hepatitis are fever (usually), an elevated white-blood-cell count, pain in the upper right abdomen, and jaundice. The disease may or may not be associated with fatty liver or cirrhosis. It usually subsides when drinking is stopped, although occasionally a patient dies of liver failure or goes on to contract cirrhosis even though he has discontinued alcohol.

One case I'm familiar with is of a hard-drinking friend who developed hepatitis over twelve years ago. He was hospitalized for several weeks and on his release his physician advised him to avoid alcohol entirely for at least two years. He stuck to teetotalism for only a couple of months, however, then went back to drinking. He is still in perfect health, despite this flouting of doctor's orders. Possibly what has kept him from any recurrence of liver trouble is the fact that he no longer drinks every day. Although still a heavy drinker, he confines his drinking to one or two days on the weekend. This intermittency of intake, allowing the liver to rest and regenerate between drinking bouts, may have been enough to keep him well. (I tell this story to illustrate the recuperative powers of the liver, *not* to urge hepatitis convalescents to follow the example of my rash friend. He was lucky—in his place many others might have suffered severe relapses.)

Cirrhosis. When damage to the liver, from whatever cause (these causes can include, besides alcohol, poor nutrition, infection, gallstone complications and heart failure), becomes so severe that scarring occurs, the result is cirrhosis. The liver ceases to function properly. The scarring produces a damming effect which impedes the flow of blood in the liver. Bypassing the liver, the circulatory system then begins to return blood directly from the intestinal tract to the general system, with the impurities that would normally be removed still present. The abdominal cavity begins to fill with fluid (dropsy). The patient's arms and legs become spindly and malnourished. In males testicles atrophy and breasts enlarge. Females suffer a cessation of menstrual periods and their breasts may either enlarge or shrink away. All these symptoms can be reversed by stopping drinking, provided the scarring has not progressed to the point where the liver is no longer able to regenerate. Once cirrhosis has become fully established, however, the disease is fatal.

How *much* drinking does it take to produce cirrhosis? The most thorough study of the relationship between alcohol intake and cirrhosis is one done by Professor G. Pequignot, of France, in 1961. Professor Pequignot's figures are as follows:

1. Harmless use of alcohol	up to 80 grams per day
	(4 ⅔ oz. 100-proof spirits)
2. Risk zone	80 to 160 grams
	(4 ⅔ to 9 ⅓ oz. of 100-proof spirits)
3. Great risk exists with	more than 160 grams
	(9 ⅓ oz. of 100-proof spirits)

According to both Pequignot and another researcher, Dr. W. K. Lelbach, of the University of Bonn, persons who drink about a pint of whiskey or more daily for twenty years stand about a 50–50 chance of developing cirrhosis. Below this level of intake, chances of cirrhosis drop sharply, although the disease has been known to strike extremely moderate drinkers occasionally.

If you're at all worried about your liver, you should go to your doctor and ask him about getting an S.G.O.T. test. S.G.O.T. (serum glutamic oxaloacetic transaminase) is a liver enzyme, the elevation of which can indicate that a mild degree of liver damage is occurring. There can be other causes for an S.G.O.T. elevation, however, so the test should be given and evaluated by a physician who is knowledgeable about its uses.

Not everyone is equally susceptible to cirrhosis. Jews, for some reason, seldom get cirrhosis. In Israel, where heavy drinking has become quite common among some segments of the population, cases of cirrhosis are seldom seen. Males with smooth, hairless chests, on the other hand, are extremely vulnerable. It used to be thought, because of a predominance of cirrhotic cadavers with hairless chests, that cirrhosis caused hair loss, but this notion, according to surgeon-author Dr. Richard Selzer of New Haven, has been proved erroneous. So if you're a man with a bathing-suit-model physique, lay off the booze!

Alcohol and Your Heart

Although alcohol does seem to provide at least some degree of protection against atherosclerosis and coronary heart disease, its role in another type of heart ailment, cardio-myopathy, is anything but helpful. Fortunately, this disease is usually confined to persons with a long history of ultra-heavy drinking. As opposed to coronary heart disease, myocardia is not due to circulatory problems but to a weakening of the heart muscle itself. The heart becomes enlarged, the neck veins distended; there is a narrow pulse pressure, elevated diastolic blood pressure, and edematous swellings of the limbs. This condition is identical to nutritional cardio-myopathy (one of the symptoms of beri-beri, caused by deficiency of the B vitamins, particularly B_1) but some researchers in recent years have attempted to show that myopathy (weakness and deterioration of the muscles) can be produced by alcohol alone. Though their arguments are not totally convincing to nutritionists (whose criteria for a "good" or "adequate" diet are rather stringent), the fact remains that cardio-myopathy is a very serious disease. Any drinker experiencing a sudden or gradual weakening of the muscles should consult a doctor or cardiologist forthwith.

The French have long congratulated themselves on their relative immunity to atherosclerosis and coronary heart disease, which they ascribe to *le bon vin*. But from Dr. Kurt Oster, Chief of Cardiology at Park City Hospital in Bridgeport, Connecticut, comes an intriguing new hypothesis which would ascribe the Frenchman's cardiac health not so much to his wine as to his *milk*. Dr. Oster believes that atherosclerosis is caused not by cholesterol-containing animal fat, but by an enzyme called xanthine oxydase. Xanthine oxydase is produced by the human liver and is normally found in certain parts of the body, but seldom in the heart or walls of arteries. The xanthine oxydase enzyme is antagonistic to these sites, and if it reaches them they will lay down atherosclerotic deposits to protect themselves. This might explain why alcoholics have a lower incidence of heart attacks than the rest of the population: Due to depressed liver function, they are not producing as much xanthine oxydase.

But Dr. Oster believes that the offending enzyme enters the system when we drink cow's milk, which contains xanthine oxydase (human milk does not). No xanthine oxydase can be absorbed from milk which has been curdled or preboiled (killing the enzyme) and only small quantities could be directly absorbed from ordinary whole milk (the enzyme particles being mostly too large to be absorbed through blood vessel walls), but when milk is *homogenized,* the smaller size of the particles enables the xanthine oxydase to enter the bloodstream and attack heart and arteries. This would seem to be an interesting theory only, were it not for the fact that heart disease does appear to increase in proportion to the consumption of whole and especially of homogenized milk.

Let's compare figures for the four nations with the most heart attacks and the four with the least.

Country	Atherosclerosis Death Rate per 100,000	Milk Consumption (in pounds per person)	Homogenized	Preboiled
Finland	244.7	593	33%	No
United States	211.8	273	almost all	No
Australia	204.6	304	15%	No
Canada	187.4	288	part	No
Switzerland	75.9	370	small quantity	Yes
Sweden	74.7	374	—	Yes
France	41.7	230	—	Yes
Japan	39.1	48	some	—

Notice that Finland, by far the largest milk consumer, leads in deaths. The United States, where virtually no unhomogenized whole milk is sold, is second. All four high-death-rate countries use unboiled whole milk. Of the four countries with low death rates, three preboil their milk and the fourth, Japan, uses cow's milk much less than do the Western nations.

Make mine buttermilk, or yogurt!

Alcohol and the Brain

A number of experiments have shown that brain damage can be induced in laboratory animals by exposure to alcohol. Apparently alcohol interferes with the metabolism of the brain in ways which we don't yet fully understand. Similar experimentation on humans is of course impossible (thankfully) but alcoholic brain damage in humans can be confirmed.

Drs. Ben Morgan Jones and Oscar A. Parsons, of the University of Oklahoma Health Services Center, recently made some experiments which confirm that chronic drinkers behave like patients with verified brain damage. To test their subjects, they gave the Halstead Category Test, a geometrical concept-forming task which measures frontal-lobe damage, to 120 adults at a Veterans Hospital. Forty of the subjects were dried-out male alcoholics, 40 patients with brain damage, and 40 a control group with no alcoholic or neurological history. They reported their experiment in an article in *Psychology Today:*

> Since older people generally don't do so well on this test as younger people, we divided each group into old and young patients. The results confirmed our original suspicion. The young alcoholics performed nearly as well as the young controls, whereas young alcoholics and young controls got better scores than the young brain-damaged patients. The older alcoholics, as expected, performed somewhat like the older brain-damaged patients, while both these groups did much worse than the older controls.
>
> We discovered that the longer a person had been an alcoholic, the more his scores suffered. The results of a later study showed that excessive drinking for more than eight years would impair a person's abstracting and conceptualizing abilities. Still another test, in which we asked alcoholics to turn a knob as slowly as possible, satisfied us that they were unable to exert as much inhibitory control over their motor behavior as were nonalcoholics.

This brain deterioration is by no means uniform for all drinkers, however. Dr. Parsons told me that while his studies have led him to believe that anyone drinking a pint of liquor a day over a period of years would probably incur significant brain damage, he has nevertheless tested quart-a-day drinkers who came through his tests with flying colors. He has no opinion on why some drinkers seem to have escaped brain damage while others succumb.

Another, though less conclusive, finding of the Jones-Parsons studies is that though long-term alcoholics are just as intelligent verbally as nonalcoholics, some aspects of their nonverbal, spatial and visual performance seem to be decidedly inferior. "This suggests that the usually dominant left hemisphere of the brain, which is primarily responsible for language, suffers less than the right hemisphere, which appears to be more responsible for nonverbal information processing, including the recognition of shapes and tones and the analysis of spatial and tactile patterns," say Jones and Parsons. In other words, a highly verbal chronic drunk may appear to be of unimpaired intelligence while actually he's deteriorated in ways that don't show.

Do "normal" drinkers get brain damage too?

There is no real answer to this question, but I don't think in general that tests made on alcoholics are necessarily "exportable" to the rest of the drinking population. The type of alcoholic used in medical experiments is someone who has demonstrated he is unable to handle liquor. He has been hospitalized, perhaps repeatedly; has spent long periods of his life in Stages Three and Four; has perhaps suffered attacks of delirium tremens and other destructive conditions; has usually lived for long periods of time with totally inadequate nutrition—in short, he has been self-destructive and has not been living a normal life.

A voice from the morgue

I asked Dr. Milton Helpern, former Chief Medical Examiner of New York City and a man who has probably conducted more autopsies than anyone else in his profession, whether he had observed signs of brain atrophy in alcoholic cadavers. He said that atrophy, not only of the frontal lobes but of the entire brain, was quite common in alcoholics. The condition is apparent by the large collection of fluid on the surface of the brain —"peel edema" (sometimes called "external hydrocephalus") —which is found when the skull is opened up. "The condition is only evident in the autopsy room. You see it on the surface of the brain when you're taking the skull cap off. Once the brain has been removed and placed in formalin for examination by a pathologist, however, evidences of atrophy can no longer be observed. This is why many pathologists, who work only on organs removed for them by technicians, are unfamiliar with alcoholic brain atrophy." Alcoholics also show lesions in the "mammillary bodies" of the brain—Wernicke's syndrome, a deterioration of the brain due to acute vitamin B_1 shortage. "There's no question that the brain suffers definite damage from alcoholism," says Dr. Helpern. "Not all alcoholics show it, of course, just as not all of them show cirrhosis or fatty liver. But many do. You see a lot of muscle atrophy, too." Dr. Helpern believes that only heavy and prolonged drinking can produce severe changes in the body. When he finds such changes in a body represented as a having been a moderate drinker, he tends to feel that the person was, in fact, an alcoholic who drank more heavily than was reported.

Avoiding the hazards

First we know that heavy drinking over a period of years is what produces serious disease in drinkers. What constitutes dangerously heavy drinking? Well, if animal experiments are any guide, drinking is most dangerous when alcohol constitutes 50 percent (or more) of the total calories in the diet. That is the ratio of alcohol to food that was successful in producing cirrhosis in baboons (previous experiments to produce cirrhosis in animals had failed because the experimenters were unable to make the animals ingest that much alcohol—when offered a liquid diet containing more than 40 percent alcohol calories, the rat, for instance, will refuse it; he'd rather starve to death). Anything approaching a 50–50 distribution between food and alcohol calories should be avoided, therefore. Probably 40 percent is too high also. An intake of two-thirds food calories to one-third alcohol calories, or less, would seem best. (See Chapter 6, "The Overweight Problem" for tables on alcohol calories.)

Second, we know that prolonged, day-after-day, year-after-year drinking of even moderate amounts can put a strain on the liver and other organs. So it would seem prudent to have a "dry" day every once in a while. New York cardiologist Dr. Elliott J. Howard, who wrote the Foreword to this book, advises patients who take three or more drinks daily to abstain completely for two days a week, ". . . to allow the organs (liver, brain, heart) and muscles to 'detoxify' from the alcohol-breakdown products. Some day, when we are able to pinpoint the exact nature of the toxic reaction, we can be more specific in our advice. Meanwhile, as a conservative precautionary health measure, periodic abstention seems a wise course."

12

"I Never Drink on Monday" and Other Ploys for Drinking Less

ONE GOOD THING about drinking heavily is that when you are a heavy drinker it's easy to cut down. If you're walking around in an alcoholic haze most of the time, feeling worn out, tired or hung over from too much booze, all you need to do is take a day off, get a good night's sleep and you'll feel *tons* better.

Let's talk about ways in which various types of drinkers can reduce their alcohol consumption, starting with the simplest type of case and proceeding to more difficult ones.

When there are no "willpower problems" or "irresistible" cravings

If overdrinking is caused by inattention or stupidity or the thoughtless habit of gulping down whatever is thrust into your hand or pouring and/or ordering yourself a drink whenever you're somewhere where liquor is available, then your problem is slight. All you need do is lessen your alcoholic consumption, in any way that seems convenient and plausible for your way of life. Here are some suggestions for when and how.

1. *Lunchtime.* If you're in the habit of having two or three drinks at lunch, have only one—or none.

2. *The cocktail hour.* Set it as late as possible. Five is good, five-thirty better, six splendid. Make it a rule never to take a drink before then. If that's not enough, you can limit the number of drinks you have—"I take two drinks before dinner, no more, no less."

3. *NO cocktail hour.* A drastic limitation, but it works. Don't drink during the day, not before dinner, not during, but only *after.* Then let 'er rip.

4. *Set aside a "dry" day or two.* Pick out a day when it's convenient to not drink and announce, to yourself and others, "I never drink on Monday (or Friday or whenever)." If that's not enough, add a second day.

5. *Become a connoisseur.* Stop buying house-brand Bourbon by the case at huge savings and get yourself a bottle or two of something really good like Beam's Choice, Maker's Mark or Wild Turkey. Sip your drinks and savor the difference. Lay off the jug wines and start experimenting with French châteaus and California varietals.

Dealing with craving

One of the great minds of our century, someone whose name I can't bring myself to mention in connection with a subject as sordid as that of this book, once said that there is no such thing as a craving *for* something. There is only craving, in general. If there is such a thing as a specific craving shared by all mankind, he went on, it is the *craving for permanency of desire.* Craving, in other words, is not wanting something, it is *wanting to want* something. In the midst of eternal chaos, our idiot minds desire permanency, security, order. One way to get these is to find something that magically always satisfies, always fulfills. This might be a steak, a cigarette, a drink, a mystical religious experience, sex, anything. Logan Pearsall Smith wrote that his idea of heaven on earth would be to read and forget, reread and reforget, endlessly, the novels of Jane Austen.

Craving has a way of making the craver more real to himself. He's not just a blah, a human cipher, a jellyfish—he *wants* something, by God! Craving can only be done in the absence of the craved object, or when that object is prohibited. Sitting in his kitchen with a refrigerator full of six-packs, a beer drinker does not crave beer. It's only when he's out in the hot sun miles from anywhere that he says to himself, "Boy, wouldn't an ice-cold Bud go good right now!" The cigarette smoker only craves a smoke when he wakes up in the middle of the night and finds he's out of cigarettes, or when he's decided to quit the smoking habit.

Another characteristic of craving is that it's an obsession, something the craver broods about constantly. Any unusual condition of the mind-body—a twinge of self-doubt, feeling of bodily discomfort, change of mood, etc.—is interpreted as a desire for the craved object. The smoker thinks he wants a smoke, the drinker a drink, the sex fiend a f——.

Craving is a form of self-brainwashing. Just as the lover will "psych" himself up for an assignation with his mistress by dwelling mentally on her charms for hours beforehand, a drinker will spend a lot of time thinking about how good the first drink of the day is going to taste. Often this is a communal activity, with several drinkers egging each other on to lust after booze, "I bet I know what George is thinking about right now. A nice tall Johnny Walker, right, George?"

In dealing with craving it's good to remember that it's unreal, a trumped-up condition you've programmed yourself into. The way to handle craving is not to resist it or give in to it, but to *experiment* with it. Say you're used to having a drink first thing when you get home from the office. You crave that drink, feel physically in need of it, look forward to it as a big event of the day. You know that that craving consists of (a) a stimulus, some sort of feeling of lack, and (b) an answer to that stimulus, such as "I need a drink."

Instead of responding to the obvious and taking a drink, try something new. Perhaps part of your "need" for a drink is simply that you're thirsty, so take a drink of water. Maybe you're feeling a little frazzled because your blood sugar is low: eat something sweet. Could be you're hungry and really crave the hors d'oeuvres that come with the drinks, so eat and don't drink. Perhaps you're tense and need to unwind; do something that will relax you: mow the lawn, shoot a game of pool, call up an amusing friend and have a long conversation, make love to your wife, read a good book, take a nap. . . . In short, feed your craving something other than booze. You may find that it's just as well satisfied, for the moment, at least.

When you do drink, pay attention to your reactions: Are you enjoying the drink, does it taste good, did you really want it, do you feel better after having had it, or worse? Are you experiencing the actual drink, or an image of some imaginary, idealized ambrosia? Many drinkers have spent so much time *pretending* to like booze that they no longer have the slightest idea whether they really enjoy drinking or not. The pretense of enjoyment is part of the drinking ritual.

How to get less drunk

In Chapter 2 we talked about the difficulties of trying to stay moderately immoderate. It's relatively easy to decide to have only one or two drinks and adhere to the decision, but how can you keep a resolve such as "I'm only going to get slightly drunk, not really drunk!" By the time you're mildly smashed the party spirit has reached you and you're impatient with that tiresome fellow, the sober boring you, who's so hung up on moderation. Ignoring *him,* you pour yourself a few more stiff ones and become thoroughly bombed.

Is it possible for Sober You to give Drunk You instructions and have him carry them out? Yes, to a certain extent, if you remember that Drunk You is a different person who doesn't have all of your awarenesses and doesn't respond, necessarily, to the same arguments you respond to. It's like sending a small child on an errand—you don't give him all sorts of complicated instructions he's liable to forget; you tell him very simply and clearly what to do. Let's say you're going to a party where you know hilarity will reign and the booze will flow very freely. You want to have *some* fun but would like to get home in reasonably viable condition. This means you can drink yourself into Stage Two but certainly not beyond. *You* know what you want, but how do you persuade the Stage Two "you" to go along with your wish?

He's not as sensible as you are, remember. You can't just say to him, "Listen here, old chap, we've been hitting the bottle entirely too much lately, and in the interest of moderation I suggest we take it easy tonight. Besides we have a nine-o'clock tennis date with Bill Ferguson tomorrow and we don't want to show up all hungover, do we? Therefore I think you ought to try to cool it as much as you can. If you notice you're getting at all out of hand during the evening, just switch to plain club soda for a while, okay?" That's no way to talk to Stage Two. He's an expansive, on-going fellow who likes to think of himself as slightly larger than life. You can ask him to perform a heroic mission, but not some niggling little act of self-denial or self-assessment. Talk to him like this, "Old buddy, I want you to do something very important for me. Very important! Listen carefully, here's what I want you to do: When you get to the party, you're to drink exactly *two drinks per hour,** no more. Got that? One drink every half hour. One at nine, one at nine-thirty, one at ten . . . is that clear? Got your watch on? Is it all wound up? Look at it *every time,* okay? You know why this is so important? Because they say we're a couple of patsies for the booze, you and I. They say we can't possibly drink and not get crocked. Well, we're going to show *them,* right? *Two drinks per hour.* Don't let me down, now. I know I'm going to be *proud* of you when the party's over."

*Or whatever other amount you calculate will keep him safely in Stage Two.

The drunken self is impatient of petty details but will attend to considerations it deems urgent or important.

Some clues from "behavior modification"

In the last few decades, behavioral psychologist B. F. Skinner and his followers have evolved a system of modifying human and animal behavior that can be used for everything from teaching pigeons to pilot missiles to re-educating autistic children to rehabilitating alcoholics—and it *works*. (The main criticism of behavior modification, in fact, is that it works *too* well, and should not be used on people without their consent.) So let's take a look at behavior mod and see if it can give us some ideas for controlling drinking.

Behavior mod is almost absurdly simple. It is concerned only with behavior, not thoughts, feelings or motivations. A behavior modification practitioner wouldn't care why you drink, for instance; he'd only be interested in how much, how often. He'd probably have you count exactly how many drinks you take each day and record the number on weekly or monthly charts. If craving for drink or obsession with drink is one of your problems, he'd have you carry around a little pocket counter and click it once every time the thought of liquor crosses your mind—how many times a day: five, ten, fifty, a hundred? These numbers too would be recorded on a chart. You would now have a quantitative picture of the behavior you want to change. Also, the mere fact of knowing the extent of the problem might produce a certain feedback and influence you to lessen your frequency of drinking or thinking about drinking.

Behavior, the mod people say, is controlled by *reinforcement*. If a certain behavior has good or pleasant or rewarding consequences, people tend to repeat it. If it has unpleasant or boring consequences, they do not. Good consequences are called positive reinforcement, bad ones negative reinforcement. One might call this reward and punishment, but that would distort the process somewhat. Reinforcement is unitary, with positive reinforcement leading to greater frequency of the reinforced behavior and negative reinforcement leading to lesser frequency and finally *extinction.* (If you had to walk three miles every time you wanted a shot of booze, you'd soon quit drinking.)

Negative reinforcement cannot produce a desired behavior; it can only extinguish an undesired one. It can produce lack of frequency of an undesired behavior, but will not produce greater frequency of an alternate, desired one.

The trouble with all this is that the world is constantly reinforcing undesirable behavior and unreinforcing the desirable. For instance, when you stay sober nobody comes up and claps you on the back and tells you what a fine fellow you are. No, they take you for granted, perhaps even act as if you're somewhat boring. But when you get smashed and make an ass of yourself, all sorts of attention is paid to you—not all favorable, to be sure, but *any* form of attention is a payoff. You may squirm as they tell you all the terrible things you did last night, but at least they're *talking* about you.

How does one work behavior modification on oneself? First, count. Keep a notebook and write down every drink you consume. *You may not have a drink unless you mark it down.* Second, make drinking more difficult. Don't keep liquor at your elbow; put it in the farthest-away room of your house, so that you have to make a trek to go get a drink. Don't have ice bucket and mixers handy to the booze, either. Put them somewhere else, so that you have to make *two* treks for each drink. Time your drinking, allowing yourself only one drink every half hour. Later lengthen that to one hour. At parties, don't walk around with your glass in your hand. Put it in some remote corner so you have to walk over to it every time you want a sip. Et cetera.

While you're doing all this, you also reward yourself for a diminishing frequency of drinking, punish yourself for an increase. Figure out appropriate rewards and punishments. For instance, when you've been good you get to buy yourself a new tie or eat out at your favorite restaurant. When you were bad you deprive yourself of watching the ball game on

Sunday, or are forced to send $5 to your least favorite charity.

Another behavior modification technique is the *contract*. Actually this is a ploy that existed long before anyone ever heard of B. F. Skinner. In its simplest form, you bet somebody you can stay sober, or quit drinking entirely, for *x* amount of time. This works even better with two people who both want to cut down or quit. The ultimate fiendish contract is when you bet another drinker $50, $100, $500—some amount that will really *hurt*—that you can stay on the wagon longer than he can.

Reinforcing the sober you

If you're trying to cut your alcohol intake, it's probably because the joys of drunkenness or semi-drunkenness are wearing a little thin for you. Drinking less is a worthy goal, but also a rather negative one. So don't dwell too much on the thought of controlling your drinking. Concentrate instead on rediscovering the joys of sobriety. Note how pleasant it is to wake up with a clear, unhungover head. Learn to enjoy having a sober mind with its alertness, its subtle interplay of thoughts and feelings too evanescent for the booze-deadened brain to apprehend. Get up early to watch a sunrise or go bird watching. Take up something that demands sobriety, such as Transcendental Meditation, solving chess problems or building ship models out of toothpicks. Spend more time with children, animals and other creatures that know how to have fun without drinking. You've explored that dark world at the bottom of the bottle long enough (and it hasn't *all* been unworthwhile) but now come out in the clear light of day!

When you feel you need help

Perhaps your drinking habit is so firmly ingrained you don't feel you can cope with it all by yourself. What should you do —go to a psychiatrist, enroll in group therapy, join AA? Here are some suggestions.

The "buddy system." Find someone else who wants to cut

down—preferably someone who's intelligent and resourceful and whose company you can tolerate—and figure out a plan whereby you can jointly achieve your goal. Perhaps this might take the form of having "sober night," in which you spend the evening together not drinking. Or you could agree on exactly how many drinks you ought to have during a party or pub crawl, with each person monitoring the other to make sure the limit is adhered to. Two willpowers are greater than one.

Drink Watchers. This is an interesting organization, rather new at this writing, which seems to have a lot of promise. Founded by former alcoholics who were interested in controlling their drinking but who felt unable to adhere to the rigorous Alcoholics Anonymous regime, Drink Watchers organizes meetings at which people who feel they have drinking problems get together for discussion and mutual aid. Their primary aim is "To put alcohol in the proper perspective in our lives, whether that be drinking moderately or totally abstaining." Drink Watchers tries to help those members who feel they *can* drink to do so in a sensible, guilt-free way. They provide information on nutrition, give advice on bringing in guest speakers (anyone from a psychiatrist to an expert on French wines), serve as an information center for all sorts of data that might be of use to drinkers with and without problems. Drink Watcher groups have been formed all over the country. Each group is autonomous. The home office serves as a link between the groups and publishes the monthly Drink Watchers' *Newsletter.* To find out more about the organization send $10 to Drink Watchers, P.O. Box 179, Haverstraw, New York 10927, for a one-year subscription to the *Newsletter* (or $1 for a single sample copy).

Behavior modification clinics. There are a number of these springing up around the country, and their approach has been shown effective in teaching people to control their drinking. One such is the Center for Behavioral Medicine at the University of Pennsylvania in Philadelphia. There's no "central registry" of behavior mod groups. If you're interested in finding one, the best way might be to ask around in the psychology department of the nearest large university. Somebody there is bound to have the information you want.

Alcoholics Anonymous. Do you feel that you're ruining your life with booze? That you *must* stop drinking but lack the power to do so on your own? That alcohol is a poison for you and that you'd be better off if you never again took a drink in your life? Then AA are the people for you. They have saved countless thousands of souls from the depths of alcoholic degradation and stand ready to do the same for you—anytime, day or night, just reach for your phone, they're in the book. They're a godsend for anyone who really needs them.

Anticlimax, or how to get more drunk on less

Getting back to the drinker who doesn't really need to quit, let me end this chapter on a frivolous note. This is for the drinker who feels he ought to drink moderately but doesn't want to because it's so boring. I mean, you can't even get a *buzz* on with two or three measly little drinks! Two suggestions. One, drink champagne. (California or New York State will do, if you're on a budget.) Due to its bubbliness, champagne is the most drunk-making substance, per gram of alcohol contained, that you can find. Or two, *gulp* your drinks. It's rather unmannerly to do that with a highball or cocktail, so switch to straight shots with a tall chaser. Down the shot in one swallow, then linger over the chaser. That way, you can make three drinks do the work of six. . . .

In Conclusion

ALCOHOL IS a neutral spirit, good or bad as we make it so. On the whole, perhaps it is bad because although it can relieve us of our crabbiness, our stiffness, our standoffishness and make us a little more cheerful and friendly, it cannot offer us any truly improved state of mind or being. And to get its benefits we must allow it to cloud our minds a little and deaden our bodies a little. Until we've learned to produce joy within our own natural minds, however, we'll probably continue to need the joy that comes inside a bottle.

So let's drink freely but not greedily. To your health, everyone!

Bibliography

ABRAHAMSON, E. M., M.D., and A. W. PEZET. *Body, Mind & Sugar,* New York: Holt, Rinehart & Winston, 1951.

BACON, SELDEN D. *Studies of Drinking and Driving, Quarterly Journal of Studies on Alcohol,* 1968.

BREAN, HERBERT. *How to Stop Drinking,* New York: Holt, Rinehart & Winston, 1958.

CAHALAN, DON *et al. American Drinking Practices,* Rutgers Center of Alcohol Studies, 1969.

COOPER, KENNETH H., M.D. *The New Aerobics,* M. Evans, 1970.

DAVIS, ADELLE. *Let's Eat Right to Keep Fit,* New American Library (paperback), 1970.

DI CYAN, ERWIN. *Vitamins in Your Life,* New York: Simon & Schuster, 1974.

FORSANDER, OLOF, and KALERVO ERIKSSON. *Biological Aspects of Alcohol Consumption,* Finnish Foundation for Alcohol Studies, 1971.

GERMANN, DONALD R., M.D. *Too Young to Die,* Farnsworth, 1974.

GREENBERG, LEON A. *Studies of Congeners in Alcoholic Beverages, Quarterly Journal of Studies on Alcohol,* 1970.

GROSSMAN, HAROLD J. *Grossman's Guide to Wines, Beers and Spirits,* New York: Charles Scribner's Sons, 1964.

HEWITT, DONALD W., M.D. *Alcoholism: a Treatment Guide for General Practitioners,* Lea & Febiger, 1957.

JELLINEK, E. M. *The Disease Concept of Alcoholism,* Hillhouse, 1960.

JOHNSON, HARRY J., M.D. *Executive Life-Styles,* New York: Thomas Y. Crowell Company, 1974.

LAMB, LAWRENCE E., M.D. *Metabolics,* New York: Harper & Row, 1974.

LEAKE, CHAUNCEY D. and MILTON SILVERMAN. *Alcoholic Beverages in Clinical Medicine,* Chicago: Yearbook Publishers, 1966.

LUCE, GAY GAER. *Body Time,* New York: Pantheon Books, 1971.

MAYER, JEAN. *Overweight: Causes, Cost and Control,* New York: Prentice-Hall, 1968.

MENDELSON, JACK H., M.D. *Experimentally Induced Chronic Intoxication and Withdrawal in Alcoholics, Quarterly Journal of Studies on Alcohol,* 1964.

MENNINGER, KARL, M.D. *Whatever Became of Sin?,* New York: Hawthorne Books, 1973.

MOREHOUSE, LAURENCE E., and LEONARD GROSS. *Total Fitness in 30 Minutes a Week,* New York: Simon & Schuster, 1975.

PEELE, STANTON, with ARCHIE BRODSKY. *Love and Addiction.* New York: Taplinger, 1974.

PFEFFER, ARNOLD Z., M.D. *Alcoholism,* Grune & Stratton, 1958.

PITTMAN, DAVID J., and CHARLES R. SNYDER. *Society, Culture and Drinking Patterns,* Southern Illinois University Press, 1973.

ROSENBERG, HAROLD, and A. N. FELDZAMEN. *The Doctor's Book of Vitamin Therapy,* New York: G. P. Putnam's Sons, 1974.

ROUECHE, BERTON. *The Neutral Spirit,* Boston: Little, Brown and Company, 1960.

SECRETARY OF HEALTH, EDUCATION & WELFARE. *Alcohol & Health, First Special Report to Congress,* 1971; *Second Report,* 1974.

SINCLAIR, ANDREW. *Era of Excess,* Harper-Colophon, 1964.

SMITH, WALTON HALL, and FERDINAND C. HELWIG, M.D. *Liquor, The Servant of Man,* Boston: Little, Brown and Company, 1940.

SUNDBY, PER. *Alcoholism and Mortality,* Oslo: Universitetsvorlaget, 1967.

SZASZ, THOMAS, M.D. *Ceremonial Chemistry,* New York: Doubleday & Company, 1974.

TURCHETTI, RICHARD J., and JOSEPH J. MORELLA. *New Age Nutrition,* Chicago: Henry Regnery Company, 1974.

WATSON, GEORGE. *Nutrition and Your Mind,* New York: Harper & Row, 1972.

WILLIAMS, ROGER J. *Nutrition Against Disease,* New York: Pitman Publishing Corporation, 1971.

_____ *Alcoholism: The Nutritional Approach,* University of Texas, 1959.

_____ *Biochemical Individuality,* New York: Pitman Publishing Corporation, 1956.

VARIOUS AUTHORS. *Aspects of Alcoholism,* Vols. I & II, Philadelphia: J. B. Lippincott Company, 1963.

Index

warmth, drinking and feeling of, 2
weekend drinkers (*see also* Social drinking), 106
weight
blood alcohol concentration (BAC) and, 4–7, 10–11
controlling, 69–84
whiskey absorption rate, 2
White, Dr. Paul Dudley, 44
wines, 2, 43–6
Williams, Dr. Roger J., 37, 48, 51–2, 58–9, 67–8

women
blood alcohol concentration (BAC) and weight, 5–7
as drunken drivers, 99
pregnant, vitamin needs, 59
Prohibition era and, 29–30
sex and alcohol, 95
Wright, Dr. Irving S., 44–5

Zylman, Richard, 98–9